Christamaria Fiedler

Spaghetti Crime

Thienemann

– 1 –

They say that disaster is always **lurking** just around the corner. But why did it always have to come at the wrong time!

Isy could only stare at her mother's leg. It was encased in a spanking new **plaster cast**. What was going to happen to the school trip to Green Meadows now? Isy knew that her mother would be **devastated** if her accident ended up ruining the Year Six trip.

The trip to **the school's** country **lodge** had had enough problems as it was. The crisis had started in the summer, when a few teachers and older students had decided to touch up the lodge with a lick of fresh paint and some brand-new wallpaper. A series of **disruptions** and delays meant that the job hadn't been finished when school began again. The Do-it-yourself specialists ended up **cutting** their assignment **short** without having cleaned up the inevitable mess. News soon spread that the lodge was

---

to lurk – lauern; plaster cast – Gipsverband; to be devastated – am Boden zerstört sein; school lodge – Schullandheim; disruption – Panne/Unterbrechung; to cut short – abbrechen

looking like a **pigsty** and the headmaster came to the logical conclusion that it was unacceptable to let the next school trip go there without first giving the place a thoroughly good clean.

In response to the crisis, a few mothers from Year Six had spontaneously offered to go to Green Meadows over the first few days of the **October half-term** and get the lodge into shape. The first mother **backed out** less than a week after her promise. A second mother soon followed, due to some family problem or other, and eventually the last-but-one mother **threw in the towel**, making some excuse about a clash with a training module at work. The only mother left over was Isy's, whose determination to keep her promise had been completely blown out of the window today. How is it possible to have so much bad luck all at the same time? Of all the mums in all the world, why did it have to be *her* mum who had to trip over Selma?

And of all the cats in all the world, why did they have to choose a *black* cat which was practically invisible in the dark **crannies** of the flat?

And why, for crying out loud, wasn't her mother wearing her new glasses at the time?

"Dad's right," said Isy, giving vent to her feelings, "you're just so **vain**! You'd have seen Selma if you'd have been wearing your glasses."

---

pigsty – Schweinestall; October half-term – Herbstferien; to back out – abspringen; to throw in the towel – das Handtuch werfen; cranny – Ecke/Winkel; vain – eitel

"Rubbish!" disagreed her mother and sighed as she hoisted her huge white leg onto the sofa. "It was just an accident, wasn't it, Selma?"

The cat on the window sill pricked up its ears and raised its head. With no sign of either a bite to eat or a pleasant interruption to her daily cat-routine, she coolly continued cleaning her shiny fur.

Go ahead, just clean yourself, thought Isy angrily. You might well have ruined everything! She thought about calling Amanda to tell her about the latest **mess** with the lodge. Things were hanging by a thread, as ever! But Amanda would be busy packing her bags, ready to leave with her parents for the sun first thing in the morning. It probably wouldn't be the best idea to start off her holidays by surprising her with this sickening news.

Anyway, it was still possible that one of the other parents would be willing to **stand in** for Isy's mother at Green Meadows. It was as if her mother could **read her mind**.

"First of all, let's call Dr. Trisch," she suggested. "Maybe he'll know what to do. I have to let him know anyway."

"Trischi's away!" announced Isy, waving her hand towards the kitchen to symbolise Denmark.

Within minutes of their last lesson her **form teacher** had jumped into his car with his wife and roared off into the half-term holidays.

---

mess – Schlamassel; to stand in – vertreten; to read sb's mind – jmds. Gedanken lesen; form teacher – Klassenlehrer

Isy's mother als einzigste mit ins Landschulheim, bei Unfall wegen Katze nicht gesehen Bein gebrochen

"He said he wasn't going to miss out on a single second of his holiday. I guess we wore him out this time."

Isy's mother laughed, but she didn't sound as happy as normal. She was obviously worried, probably because of the new job which the **job centre** had finally arranged for her a few weeks ago after months of hanging around at home. At last a new job which she enjoyed and suited her abilities. And now this had to happen!

"Can you pass me the telephone book, please?" asked her mother, interrupting her thoughts. "I mean, not everybody from school can be on holiday! Someone's **bound to** stand in for me!"

Isy dragged the three yellow books and positioned them within easy reach of her mother. Then she started pacing restlessly through the flat thinking about how the whole class had been looking forward to building a **feeding trough** for the forest deer. Trischi had not only got hold of a detailed construction manual on how to build it, but had also arranged to get the **timber** for free from the forestry office. The local ranger even wanted to give the class two talks about 'forest life'. And now all of that was just going **to go down the drain**?

Just then, Isy heard the corridor door slam. That would be her dad.

---

job centre – Arbeitsamt; to be bound to do – garantiert etw. tun müssen; feeding trough – Futterraufe; timber – Bauholz; to go down the drain – vor die Hunde gehen

Isy Landschulheim

Isys mutter gebrochener Fuß, wenn keine andere Mutter, Isy's Landschulheim fällt aus

She ran up to the new arrival, but it turned out to be Benedikt. "Hey," called Isy. "Guess who's broken a leg?"

Her brother took off his helmet and, preparing himself for the worst, ran his fingers through his hair. His hair was just as dark and curly as Isy's, and sometimes people thought they were twins. Whenever Isy heard this, she would roll her eyes and cross herself. It was enough them being brother and sister, let alone twins. He wasn't all that great!

"Broken a leg?" he asked, **gobsmacked**. "Dad?"

"No. He's out picking up the **crutches**!"

"That just leaves Mum," said her brother, dismayed. "Are you serious?"

Isy nodded very seriously. Benedikt took a deep sigh and pulled down the zip on his coat.

"**I can't be doing with this**, I can tell you!"

"Do you think Mum can be doing with it either? Now, of all times, with the new job? Or me? You know she was planning to go to Green Meadows for our school trip. If she can't find anyone to clean up the lodge, we can forget our trip!"

"I wouldn't worry about it," mumbled Benedikt, "the school lodge is **naff** anyway! Is she in bed?"

"No, on the sofa!"

Furious, Isy followed her brother into the sitting room where they gathered around the mater-

---

gobsmacked – verdutzt; crutch – Krücke; I can't be doing with this – das passt mir nicht; naff – bescheuert

nal plaster cast as if it were a holy shrine. So, all of a sudden Benedikt thought the school lodge was naff? He used to have quite a different opinion before! Why the sudden change?

Isy's mother had just finished her latest telephone call, and she didn't look too happy.

"The whole world's either on holiday, packing their bags to go on holiday, or have other plans," she told them **despondently**. "The only person who might still be able to help is Mrs Niemann. She's going to call back. Her husband promised." Then she gave her son a hug and told him about the accident.

Disappointed, Isy dropped into an armchair. 'The lama' as their last chance? Isy felt dizzy just thinking about it!

Mrs Niemann was the mother of Jennifer, the girl who'd been sitting next to Isy since Year One. Isy didn't like Mrs Niemann one bit. The worst thing about her was that she **spat** when she talked. But then again, if she did rescue Year Six's school trip, Isy would generously be able to overlook her tendency to gush when she spoke.

But unfortunately Mrs Niemann wasn't able to rescue Year Six. She had her driving test the following week and needed the time for some intensive preparation.

When Mrs Niemann called Isy's mother back, Isy was in the kitchen, packing away the shopping

---

despondent – niedergeschlagen; to spit – spucken

with her father. In his state of utter despair he'd **gone a bit over the top** in the supermarket, as if the family were about **to hibernate** for the entire winter.

"Er, Mum said I should tell you that Green Meadows is an absolute no-no!" chirped Benedikt in a tone of voice that Isy couldn't stand. "Don't take it too hard. Take it *easy*!" Man, why did he always have to make those stupid jokes about her name?

All of a sudden Isy was both furious and stunned at the same time. Strange, considering she had been preparing herself for the bad news. But for some reason or other she'd been clinging to the hope that a miracle would happen. At least now she knew how Jelly Baby must have felt when his **appendix** burst in the middle of a maths class. Awful. Everybody in the class would hate her now. Her or her mother. **Dire** stuff! There just had to be a way out of this. Before Isy could think of one, the telephone rang.

"That'll be one of the mums!" cried Isy, rushing out into the corridor.

But it wasn't some mum on the end of the line. It was Amanda.

"Yo," said Amanda, sounding like she was about to die from a cold. "Guess what happened?" she coughed into the telephone.

"What?" asked Isy, out of breath.

---

to go over the top – übertreiben; to hibernate – Winterschlaf halten; appendix – Blinddarm; dire – schrecklich, mies

"My dad broke his arm. Right in front of the travel agent's. He was just about to pay."

"That's unbelievable!" cried Isy in utter astonishment.

"You bet it is!" coughed Amanda. "So much for Gran Canaria. **Another one bites the dust!** We're staying home."

"Amanda", whispered Isy, her voice almost squeaking with excitement. "There's more dust than you think!"

"What are you talking about?"

"The school trip's **up the creek** as well!"

For a moment Isy could hear nothing but silence on the end of the line. Then Amanda uttered a deep sigh.

"**Are you out of your mind**, or what?"

"I wish I were!"

"But why?"

"Because my mum broke her leg this morning. She tripped up over Selma."

"I don't believe it!" stammered Amanda, who seemed to be completely **overwhelmed** by the day's events. "Things like that don't even happen in Hollywood! But someone's bound to be able to stand in for your mum, aren't they?"

"That's what you think! No one's got any time!"

Another one bites the dust! – Und wieder beißt einer ins Gras; to be up the creek – im Eimer sein; Are you out of your mind? – Spinnst du?; overwhelmed – überwältigt

For a moment they both fell into a stunned silence.

Then Amanda vented her disappointment. "I always thought you East Germans were different! I thought you guys didn't always just think of yourselves."

"We learn quickly," countered Isy. She didn't like it when Amanda gave her all that West German **lip**. But actually Amanda was right. People hadn't been so selfish before. Maybe just because they hadn't **dared**.

"And what about you? You always have a **brainwave**!" Amanda wouldn't give up. "You're usually bubbling with bright ideas. Come on!"

"Looks like I bubbled over," **conceded** Isy gloomily. "The only thing we can do with our school trip now is dream about it."

Isy's Mutter, Amandas Vater angebrochen Bein gebrochen!
Landschulheim fällt wahrscheinlich aus. Benedikt, Isy's Bruder, froh.

---

to dare to do sth – etw. wagen; lip – Geschwätz;
brainwave – Geistesblitz; to concede – zugeben/kapitulieren

– 2 –

That same night Isy did, in fact, have a dream. She found herself sitting in a train opposite Amanda. Her best friend was dressed in the same clothes she'd been wearing on the last day of school before half-term: baggy jeans, the black pullover which she had knitted herself, and her black and white Palestinian scarf to keep her **sore throat** warm.

What were they doing sitting in this train, and where were they heading for? "Where shall we go?" asked Isy, but Amanda didn't reply. It was almost as if her friend couldn't hear her. She looked straight through Isy as if she were made of glass. Amanda only ever did that when they'd had a nasty **tiff**. Isy felt a certain anxiety growing inside her. What was the matter with Amanda? Where was this damned train taking them? "I want to get out of here!" cried Isy and she jumped up from her seat. "I want to get out right now! Stop the train!"

The people in the **compartment** turned and stared curiously at her. Just then an announcement

---

sore throat – entzündeter Hals; tiff – Streit;
compartment – Zugabteil

bellowed over the loudspeakers: "The next station is the SCHOOL LODGE!"

Isy dropped back into her seat **with relief**. "Why didn't you tell me we were only going to Green Meadows?" she asked her best friend. But Amanda's seat was empty.

That was when Isy woke up from her dream. What was going on? Where was she? Confused, she tried to bring some clarity into the chaos left by her dream, but before she was able to do so, she rolled onto her side and fell back to sleep.

When she woke up the next morning she was **convinced** she hadn't dreamt anything at all.

She got up reluctantly. The thought of the ruined school trip already spoilt her day before it had started. She was the last member of her family to disappear into the bathroom with its customary morning smells of toothpaste, soap and cast-off sleep. As usual, the first thing Isy did was look in the mirror. The mirror reflected the image of a girl with a serious face and a **frown**. Was that supposed to be *her*? Interesting! At least her **sorrow** had a good side. It made her look older. With a face like that and shoulder-length hair she could easily pass for fourteen!

As every morning, the first thing she did was wash away Benedikt's disgusting **spot cream** from

---

with relief – erleichtert; to be convinced – überzeugt sein;
frown – Stirnrunzeln; sorrow – Kummer;
spot cream – Pickelsalbe

the brim of the **sink** and fill it with cold water. She thought of Amanda. Right now her best friend should have been sitting in a plane heading towards Gran Canaria. The reality was that she was sitting at home because of her father's broken arm. It really was a strange **coincidence** that, yesterday of all days, Isy's mum and Amanda's dad should both end up in plaster. When Isy finally turned up at the breakfast table, Benedikt was in the middle of reading out the day's horoscope from the morning paper.

"Listen up! Star sign 'Gemini'!" he smirked at her. "Pay particular attention to your dreams today! They will give you an important **clue** to solving an existing problem!"

Her dreams? Did she even have a dream last night? Isy gave her mother a kiss and slapped a huge green lump of Kiwi jam onto a slice of toast.

"Did you dream anything last night?" she asked her mother, who was stirring her coffee wearily, her white, cumbersome leg resting on a stool. Selma was lying in a pool of sunlight beside the plaster cast, **purring** contentedly.

"Me?" retorted her mother. "I couldn't get a wink of sleep with this lump on my leg. It's going to take some getting used to!"

"I didn't dream anything either," declared Isy with her mouth full. "Where's Dad?"

Her father had already left for the office to

---

sink – Waschbecken; coincidence – Zufall; clue – Hinweis;
to purr – schnurren

arrange to take his remaining holiday. He wanted to stay at home for the next few days to look after his wife. On the way back he was planning to go via the station to return the train ticket which Isy's mother would have used on the midday train.

Midday train? Station? That **rang a** few **bells**...

Slowly a few blurry images began to float back to the surface of Isy's memory. Didn't she have a strange dream about being in a train with Amanda heading for some weird-named station like SCHOOL LODGE? Yes, that was it. She had dreamt after all!

But where was the all-important clue in this crazy **hotchpotch** of a dream meant to be?

Isy was just reaching into the bread basket for a second slice of toast when it hit her like a rocket. That was it! Why hadn't she thought of that before? She jumped up from the breakfast table with such energy that Selma took off at top speed.

"Bitten by a snake?" babbled Benedikt with his mouth full of muesli. It was his own fault. If he hadn't read out the daily horoscope, then she would still be eating her breakfast in peace.

Isy dialled Amanda's number. It seemed an eternity before her best friend answered.

"Amanda, are you there?" cried Isy. "**Hold on tight!** I've had the best idea this century!"

"At this time in the morning?" grunted Aman-

---

sth rings a bell – etw. kommt jmd. bekannt vor;
hotchpotch – Kuddelmuddel; Hold on tight! – Halt dich fest!

da sleepily. "What kind of idea's that supposed to be?"

"I've just thought of who could stand in for my mum!"

"Really? Who?"

"There are two potential candidates."

"*Two* potential candidates?" echoed Amanda, slowly waking up. "Cool! Who then?"

"Us two!" said Isy cheerfully.

Isy geträumt, Amanda sitzt neben ihr, beachtet sie nicht. verschwindet auf einmal, wacht auf

Erzählt Amanda sie könnten als Betreuer mitgehen.

– 3 –

Okay, admittedly it was once again a case of Isy leaning **brazenly** on her best friend, but even she didn't believe Amanda would be standing there on time at the station the next day.

Yet the miracle had happened, and there they were, sitting with their baggage in the half-empty midday train to Green Meadows. They had made themselves comfortable opposite each other by the window. Two women were sharing the compartment with them, chatting quietly about the increase in rental prices, growing criminality and some neighbour called Loderbusch who had just bought his third new car since **the Wall** came down.

Amanda was wearing the same jeans, the same pullover and the same black and white scarf which she had been wearing in Isy's dream. But Isy hadn't told her about either the dream or the horoscope. She found both far too **embarrassing** to mention. She preferred it if people just thought she was a genius.

---

brazenly – schamlos; the Wall – die (Berliner) Mauer; embarrassing – peinlich

As soon as the train had set off, Amanda had entrenched herself behind a thick magazine and only occasionally poked her head out to blow her nose with all her might. Opposite her, Isy had buried herself in the Parking Lot **thriller**, which she'd **nicked** from her dad's bedside table. With bated breath she followed the mysterious murder of Mrs Robson in a newly built shopping centre in an old English town in the county of Sussex.

Of course, she had **suspected** Mrs Sanders' son from the very beginning, but he was becoming suspiciously over-suspicious. He probably had nothing to do with the whole thing and was cleverly written in by the author as a **red herring**.

Isy knew perfectly well what Amanda was greedily **devouring** in her opposite corner: the latest reports about the Royal Family. After Amanda had joined Isy's class two years ago, it had soon become clear that she belonged to the self-declared fan club of the British Royal Family, whose dealings, thanks to numerous intimate **publications**, Amanda **knew inside-out**. Sometimes she was on Charles's side, sometimes on Diana's, but most of all she hated the Princess' rival, Camilla Parker Bowles.

At first Isy had thought the new girl from the

---

thriller – Krimi; to nick – klauen (umgangssprachlich);
to suspect – verdächtigen; red herring – falsche Fährte;
to devour – verschlingen; publication – Veröffentlichung;
to know sth inside out – etw. bis ins kleinste Detail kennen

West and her hobby were utterly ridiculous. In the days behind the Wall, the 'anti-fascist protection barrier', people hadn't had much to do with kings, princes or princesses.

Over the past two years Isy had got to know Amanda a lot better and come to appreciate her as a friend. But for Isy Kings & Co. still belonged to the realm of **fairy tales**.

Isy's nose began to twitch at the smell of freshly baked cake. She looked up inquisitively. The two elderly ladies had begun to unwrap their provisions and were recommending the tasty cream cake to each other. Then they politely held out the packet of goodies for the girls.

Amanda fished out a petit-four, while Isy took a slice of the highly praised cream cake.

It was the cue to start a conversation: cake for information.

It started with a friendly 'where are you from?' and 'where are you going?' – the usual **chatter** between fellow travellers – and the whole time the women kept calling the girls 'Miss'. Eventually Amanda interrupted their stubborn politeness with a mouthful of pastry crumbs and a bashful smile and said: "No need to call us 'Miss'. We're only in Year Six."

"Only in Year Six?" the two ladies echoed, as if talking from the same mouth. They stared at Amanda's brightly painted fingernails and the lilac

---

fairy tale – Märchen; chatter – Geschwätz/Geplauder

eye shadow on her round face with new, disapproving eyes. "And your parents let you travel alone?"

"We're not alone," said Isy. "We're meeting up with Mrs King who has the keys for the school lodge. My parents sent her a telegram yesterday."

Following this brief **explanation** Isy went to the toilet. On her way back she took a stroll through the train and peered into other compartments. At one point she saw a **mongrel dog** in the corridor sitting next to his owner, who was smoking. She stroked the dog's grey wiry hair. "How are you doing, you passive smoker?" she said affectionately.

The dog's owner looked at Isy somewhat surprised. Then he looked at his dog and then at the burning cigarette in his hand.

"Is that true, Alfredo? Am I turning you into a co-smoker?"

There was not a trace of **ridicule** in his voice. He was summing up the situation earnestly. Isy liked him for that already.

"Your dog can't answer for himself," she said politely. "But don't you agree?"

The stranger smiled, slightly amused. "It's certainly worth thinking about!"

They chatted for a bit about dogs. The man had a moustache and rather thin hair. At the end of the

---

eye shadow – Lidschatten; explanation – Erklärung;
mongrel dog – Mischlingshund; ridicule – Spott

day, he informed Isy, people weren't the only creatures to have bad **habits**: Alfredo, for instance, liked chewing on his owner's blue sneakers. Isy saw the strangely jagged edges at the bottom of the man's shoes.

Then she went back to her compartment. Amanda had already returned to Buckingham Palace and their fellow travellers were busying themselves with some handiwork. For a while Isy watched the passing fields of the Mark Brandenburg countryside with their radiant autumn colours. Then she remembered that she'd left her camera at home. **Blast!** And she'd been planning to take some great snapshots for the **class noticeboard** as well! Just then one of the women looked up from her handiwork and glanced at her watch. "Didn't you two want to get out at Green Meadows? We're going to be there in a minute."

Isy thanked her for the prompt and stuffed her Parking Lot novel into her bag. Amanda also took her leave of the Royals and closed the magazine with a **yawn**. "By now I'd be in the sea on Gran Canaria."

Then they put on their coats and took their luggage. On top of her huge blue suitcase, Amanda had brought a **holdall** and a number of plastic bags with her. Isy's eyes had almost popped out of her head when she saw her in Berlin. What on earth was she

---

habit – Gewohnheit; Blast! – Verdammt!; class noticeboard – Wandzeitung; yawn – Gähnen; holdall – Reisetasche

taking with her? Did she think she was going to a five-star hotel?

"I can carry a bit of your household if you want," she offered generously. After all, she'd only brought **the absolute necessities** with her.

"Yeah, maybe you could take Aeschylus!" said Amanda and thrust a plastic bag into Isy's hand. "But be careful!"

"What?! You've brought your cactus with you?" cried Isy, **dumbfounded**.

"Pourquoi pas?" asked Amanda, who claimed that French had been the official language of the English monarchy for longer than English itself. "It's been to Rome, Amsterdam, Provence and Rügen. Why shouldn't it come with us to Green Meadows?" she said **pouting**, ready for a fight.

She was probably right there. Aeschylus seemed to be a true globetrotter.

They said goodbye to the two ladies, who wished them a pleasant holiday, and stepped into the corridor. Isy held the cactus cautiously away from her body so that she wouldn't be pricked through the plastic bag. The station which they were slowly pulling into was indeed Green Meadows, and they left the train with most of the other passengers.

Isy and Amanda fahren mit Zug zur Mrs King, um Schlüssel für Schatz[illegible] zu holen.

---

the absolute necessities – das absolut Notwendige; dumbfounded – entgeistert/verblüfft; to pout – die Lippen spitzen/schmollen

– 4 –

Tales about **haunted castles** in the Carpathian Mountains couldn't have been more **mysterious** than the stories which the older students had brought back with them from the school lodge in Green Meadows.

They told of bloodthirsty **bats**, like tiny vampires, flattering about on mild summer evenings; **owls darting** into their nests in the old fireplaces; and in the attic, which was permanently locked, a woman, who appeared to be no more than white mist, got up to her foul deeds. What's more, in the cellar **treasures** lay hidden, buried by three robbers.

One of the storytellers spoke of bars of pure gold, another whispered about a **magic cap of invisibility**. That sounded like a good idea, thought Isy. Whoever owned the magic cap could take as many gold bars as he could manage to drag out of the bank safes throughout the whole wide world. Quite apart from all the money.

---

haunted castle – Spukschloss; mysterious – geheimnisvoll;
bat – Fledermaus; owl – Eule; to dart – huschen;
treasure – Schatz; magic cap of invisibility – Tarnkappe

"What would you prefer to find in the cellar?" she asked her best friend as they plodded along the village high street towards the school lodge at the end. "The cap or the gold?"

"Stuffed beef with red cabbage!" puffed Amanda. The blue suitcase banged against her knees at her every step.

The way things were looking, Amanda would have put up with it for quite a while. Green Meadows was turning out to be as long as an airport **runway**. It lay tranquilly between the fields and forests, meadows and lakes of Mark Brandenburg. The houses were modest. Most of them had low-lying tiled roofs to protect them against the rain and the wind.

Isy spotted a butcher's and a baker, a tiny supermarket and a shabby, grey building with the sign POST OFFICE over the door.

At the edge of the village they eventually reached the massive, picturesque red-brick **ranger's** lodge which they recognised from Trischi's snapshots. On the other side was a forest. Isy had imagined it to be somewhat bigger. How were the whole of Year Six meant to **fit in** there?

At first sight Isy and Amanda could see that the painting group of older students had given the weather-beaten **shutters** a lick of paint during their summer expedition. One of the shutters had come

---

runway – Landebahn; ranger – Förster; to fit in – hineinpassen; shutter – Fensterladen

out of its hinges, probably because of the autumn wind. It rattled and banged against the wall of the house. This was the only sound to greet them. "Do you think Mrs King is waiting for us?" asked Amanda as she pushed open the garden gate.

"Sure she is. The telephone lines were down again, but my parents made sure they sent her a telegram." Isy looked for a bell at the gate, but couldn't find one, so she headed straight up to the front door, passing the white and reddish-brown chrysanthemums which had been neatly planted on both sides of the flagstone path. Just as she was about to knock on the weathered oak door, she spotted a handwritten **note**. Someone had **sellotaped** it next to the doorknob. The words on the small squared paper, which had probably been torn out of a maths book, read: "Please contact Mrs King, 104 High Street".

Amanda read the message as well. She dropped her luggage resolutely onto the steps. "I'm not **traipsing** all the way back there! I'm **whacked**!" She sat down on her suitcase and shook the sand out of her sneakers.

"I thought we were going to do everything together?" snapped Isy, exasperated. "That's a great start!"

She **scrutinised** Amanda, sitting there stubbornly on her monster suitcase with her legs apart,

---

note – Zettel; to sellotape – festkleben; to traipse – latschen; whacked – müde/kaputt; to scrutinise – mustern

waiting for Isy to set off all by herself. The truth was Amanda was a **weed**. Too many noodles. Too little exercise. Completely out of shape.

Isy slipped the rucksack off her back and dropped it down next to Amanda together with the sports bag and Aeschylus.

"The least you can do is look after my things!"

Then she turned around without waiting for a reply and went straight back to the village High Street.

She hadn't walked far when she heard Amanda trudging up behind her.

"Are you out of your mind? Leaving our luggage alone like that?"

"I hid it in the garden."

What? In somebody else's garden? But Isy didn't have time to get **worked up** about her friend. She was already standing in front of the house number 104. It was an old building with a new **extension** made of timber and glass. The name KING was inscribed over the doorbell in brass letters.

Isy pressed the bell.

For a while nothing happened. What were they supposed to do now? Waste their time knocking on the door here as well? The neighbours' dog started **barking** huskily. It sounded like a sheep dog in early retirement. Eventually the veranda door opened slightly. A boy looked out and eyed them up with

---

weed – Schlaffi; to be worked up – sich aufregen;
extension – Vorbau; to bark – bellen

dark, scornful eyes. His long, black hair was tied back in a **ponytail**, and he was wearing a bright red polo neck sweater. Isy hadn't been expecting to bump into such a **wacky** guy as that here.

"What do you want?"

"We'd like to speak to Mrs King."

"My mum's away."

It couldn't be true! Mrs King was away? Had anyone actually received the telegram?

"But we need the key to the school lodge!" cried Isy hastily. The guy in the red polo neck looked like he was about to disappear into the house like a **cuckoo** into its clock. "We can't get in without it, know what I mean!?"

The door opened a bit.

"My mum said two women were coming from Berlin!"

"That's right. But something went wrong. One of them had to do a training module at work, and the other one broke her leg."

The boy hesitated for a moment. Then he reached back into the veranda, picked out a **key ring** and threw it casually in their direction. Isy's hand shot out in a flash, but for some incomprehensible reason, Amanda caught it. Strange, normally she was a complete **slow coach**.

"The big one's for the front door and the other one's for the cellar and the attic!"

---

ponytail – Pferdeschwanz; wacky – blöd; cuckoo – Kuckuck; key ring – Schlüsselbund; slow coach – lahme Ente

"Merci!" called Isy, trying to sound really sophisticated, before Amanda could shoot off another French phrase. But she found herself just staring at a shut door.

They set off back to the school lodge in silence. Only once did Amanda scoff scornfully: "What a **smart arse**, huh?" And Isy had to agree with her: **"Mega-smug!"**

When they arrived back at the lodge, they dragged their luggage out of the thorny juniper bush and tried the key to the front door. When they finally managed to open it, they were met by a very unusual surprise – the hall looked like a bomb had hit it! That's how Isy's grandma, Dore Schütze, would have described the chaos which they here encountered. Speechless they found themselves staring at a pile of pots, ladders, tubs, buckets, brushes and rolls of wallpaper. The smell of fresh paint was hideous, and it was freezing cold.

"Freeze! Don't move!" Amanda coughed, horrified. "We were never here. We never touched anything. Let's get out of here, Isolde!"

---

smart arse – eingebildeter Affe; mega-smug – obereingebildet

– 5 –

There were some people who said that the West Germans would immediately throw in the towel as soon as the first problems arose. Isy's father had been working with people from Hamburg since the Wall came down and she knew from him that this always **depended on** the person, not the part of Germany they came from. Thanks to living in an economy of short supply for forty years, East Germans had the advantage of being masters in improvisation.

"Oh, come on! It'll soon be as **cosy** as anything in here!" assured Isy, pushing her friend into the house. "We just have to put plenty of **coal** on."

"Coal?" asked Amanda, horrified. "I've never used coal in my life."

No surprise there, thought Isy. It was just as well she'd learnt how to heat with coal in the simple Finnish **huts** where she and her family used to spend their holidays. That was in the Erz Mountains in Saxony, not in sunny Spain, and the sum-

---

to depend on sth – von etw. abhängen; cosy – gemütlich; coal – Kohle; hut – Hütte mer evenings there were pretty fresh. A fire was always welcome.

After they'd fought their way through the chaos in the hall to use the telephone and inform their families that they'd arrived safely in Green Meadows, Isy skilfully **kindled a** roaring **fire** in the old boiler in the cellar. In one or two years' time Green Meadows would at long last be connected to the natural gas network, and heating would no longer be a problem for anyone. While Isy heaped on the first lumps of coal and patiently waited for them to start glowing, Amanda inspected the house in search of a television, shivering from the cold. She'd already decided that she would leave this ghastly lodge that very same day if there was no television. After all, she wasn't stupid!

Eventually she found a television in the **recreation room**. It was under a sheet protecting it from the paint which had sprayed off the ceiling and walls. Amanda pulled off the sheet and turned it on. A picture came straightaway. At least something worked around here!

Feeling somewhat reconciled, she hauled the luggage up to the bedrooms on the top floor. The bedrooms all had **bunk beds**, and Amanda decided to take the smallest room at the end of the corridor for her and Isy. Saskia, Liane, Binette and Sophie would join them here when they came later. Then

---

to kindle a fire – ein Feuer anzünden;
recreation room – Aufenthaltsraum; bunk bed – Etagenbett

Amanda looked for a good spot for Aeschylus and went down to the cellar to find Isy and **complain**.

"It's still freezing cold!"

"Then put on another pullover. You've got enough clothes with you to sink a battleship!" Isy **poked** the coals, annoyed. What did Amanda expect? She couldn't perform miracles! Besides, the house hadn't been heated for months.

"And what about food?" probed Amanda further.

Yes, what about a hot meal? Only now that Amanda mentioned it did Isy started to feel a slight **rumble** in her stomach. She'd forgotten that she ought to eat something. Their parents had given them money to buy things from the supermarket, but the shops closed earlier in the country than in the city. They wouldn't have time to go shopping now.

"Have a look if there's anything in the kitchen!"

Isy's experience in holiday homes had taught her that the **predecessors** nearly always left food behind. You could usually count on left-over cornflakes, tomato puree and herbal tea, but you could often find sugar cubes, rusk bread and mustard as well. She once found a whole box of chocolate marshmallows in the kitchen of one of the holiday homes she was staying at. And another time

---

to complain – sich beschweren; to poke – herumstoßen; rumble – Knurren; predecessor – Vorgänger

Benedikt stumbled across a huge packet of Frolic, which he probably would have been really happy about if he had been a dog.

Isy heaped more coal into the boiler and soon the **pipes** began to creak and crack throughout the house. Back upstairs she found Amanda bustling away at the kitchen **stove** with a bright red face.

The results of her search for food through the pantry and kitchen cupboards were lying on the table: an opened packet of ready-made pancake flour, four wrinkly apples, half a bottle of oil, two small blotchy onions, sugar, black tea and the remains of some red cherry jam. Amanda had **taken the bull by the horns** and had already whipped up a pancake mix which she now poured carefully into the spitting fat of the pan and started to fry golden brown on both sides.

In another frying pan she had an apple-sugar-mix simmering. "Since when have you been able to cook?" asked Isy, amazed.

"Since I started ten minutes ago!" sighed Amanda. "Luckily the cooking instructions are on the packet. Or would you prefer to go hungry?"

Then she tossed the first pancake boldly onto Isy's plate and covered it generously with the stewed apple-sugar sauce. It tasted out of this world.

After the second pancake Isy had already start-

---

pipe – Rohr; stove – Herd;
to take the bull by the horns – den Stier bei den Hörnern packen

ed seeing Amanda Bornstein from a completely new perspective. In Isy's eyes her best friend could all too often be as **sluggish** as a **snail**, but now she had passed the **acid test**. Unfortunately Isy couldn't manage a third pancake.

After dinner Amanda, who was beginning to enjoy her new role in the kitchen, served a hot, black tea with the remaining jam. She boldly called it 'Tea à la Moscou'. She could just as well have called it 'Bielefeld Tea' or 'Green Meadows Tea'. Isy would have given her okay to any of them. The tea tasted absolutely delicious and it warmed up her feet, too. At the same time the heating also began to slowly creep up out of the cellar into the **radiators** on the top floor.

Their bellies full and content, the girls wandered over to the recreation room. The floor was splattered with blotches of yellow paint and looked like a field of **buttercups**. All the chairs were stacked on the tables. They took down two chairs and sat down in front of the television. They'd start with the Big Clean Up in the morning.

The regional news flickered across the screen. Isy could have hugged the entire world. They'd made it! They'd arrived in the school lodge and it felt like another planet. The old forester's house was simply fantastic. Amanda's pancakes were fantastic, life was fantastic, and the most fantastic

---

sluggish – träge; snail – Schnecke; acid test – Feuerprobe; radiator – Heizkörper; buttercup – Butterblume

thing of all was being with a friend like Amanda in Green Meadows.

No, it wasn't at all fantastic being with Amanda in Green Meadows! Why, when of all days RTL were showing a new episode of 'Columbo', did Amanda have to want to watch some wishy-washy Austrian romantic movie on another channel...?

For a while they just kept tearing the **remote control** away from each other, but they were both too tired to **squabble** for too long. After having consumed half a thriller and half a romantic movie, they eventually went to bed.

"I'm not going to let that happen again!" declared Isy from underneath her warm blanket. "From now on we share the evening between romance and murder. Sometimes it's your turn, sometimes mine. Deal?"

But Amanda didn't reply from her top bunk bed. She'd already drifted into the world of dreams.

Isy lay awake for a while before she also fell asleep, but in the middle of the night a strange **scratching** sound woke her up. What was that? Where on earth was she? And why was it so dark in here? The memory slowly came back. Oh, yes! They were in the school lodge. But there was still a strange noise coming from somewhere! It sounded like someone was **sawing down** the front door.

"Amanda," whispered Isy. "Amanda, wake up!"

---

remote control – Fernbedienung; to squabble – zanken;
to scratch – kratzen; to saw down – an etwas herumsägen

Amanda woke up at once. She didn't seem to have any problem orientating herself.

"What's up?"

"Someone's sawing down the front door!"

"It's the wind."

"But there isn't any wind!"

Isy jumped out of bed and fished around for her **slippers**. She thought of the telephone in the hallway. At least she could call the police.

"Give me the **torch**!" she hissed at Amanda.

"What torch?"

"Don't tell me you didn't bring a torch with you?"

"What about you? Did *you* bring one with you?"

Amanda could give as good as she got. Isy didn't try to reply. Without saying a word she **fumbled around** in her rucksack until she found what she was looking for. It wasn't a torch, but it was something that could eventually be of use to her.

She quietly **groped her way** down the dark corridor and crept to the top of the stairs. She could now hear the noise more clearly. It sounded more like a grating or scraping, and it didn't seem to be coming from the front door. It was in the recreation room. That made sense. There was a glass door in the recreation room which opened directly onto a terrace and the back garden. That was by far the

---

slipper – Pantoffel; torch – Taschenlampe; to fumble around – herumtasten; to grope one's way – sich vorwärts tasten

best way for a **burglar** to break into the house. He could get from the street to the terrace door completely unobserved. Isy **cautiously** started to go down the stairs. Her eyes had just about adjusted to the dark by now, but she didn't know her way around the steps, corners and crannies of the house. In the hallway it was a miracle she didn't bump into a pot of paint or stumble over a ladder.

She eventually reached the door to the recreation room. All of a sudden she heard light **footsteps** behind her.

"It's me!" whispered Amanda. "I can hear it, too. Why don't we call the police?"

"Maybe he'll run off if we turn on the light?"

"Don't start playing the **hero** now!" whinged Amanda. "It's bad enough as it is."

Before Isy could reply, they heard a slight cough from the terrace. Then there was a loud rattle.

"Isy!" whined Amanda. "I'm scared!"

"Give over! We'll turn on the terrace lights and the guy will take a running jump!"

Isy was talking, as it were, from experience. Her grandma, Dora Schütze, had a weekend house near Berlin which was constantly surrounded by various bad vibrations. And Dora Schütze said nothing was better than light!

Isy strode through to the recreation room **resolutely** and turned on the outside lights. The ter-

---

burglar – Einbrecher; cautiously – vorsichtig; footstep – Schritt; hero – Held; resolutely – entschlossen

race and back garden were immediately flooded in a bright light. Isy screwed up her eyes and scanned the scene, but try as she might, she couldn't make anything out. No one sprang startled into the night, no shadowy figure slipped into the bushes. All was still and quiet, as if she'd been dreaming.

Just as she was about to turn out the lights, the noise returned. A puffing and scratching, and a shrill clanking of metal. What was going on?

Before Amanda could stop her, Isy tore open the terrace door. It was more an impulse than an act of **courage**, and it was certainly rash, but after it had happened, Isy wished the door would slam straight back shut again. What she saw was so embarrassing. She had caught the **intruder**.

He was small, round like a ball and **prickly**. His nose had led him to the frying pan with the remains of Amanda's pancake. He was tucking in hungrily.

"A **hedgehog**!" cried Amanda with relief and glared angrily at her friend. "And you **made** such **a** big **fuss** about it?"

"Me? I didn't make a fuss! What else are you supposed to do when you hear a noise at night?"

"But you always see ghosts before you even know what's going on! It's all because of your stupid thrillers."

"A ghost? Give me a break! Did you know hedgehogs coughed?"

---

courage – Mut; intruder – Eindringling; prickly – stachlig; hedgehog – Igel; to make a fuss – einen Aufstand machen

"Of course I did."

"Oh, don't give me that! Why were you **shaking** so much then?"

Amanda was about to answer her back, and was still looking for a good argument, when she suddenly saw the weapon in Isy's hand.

"What? You've got a **piece**?" she cried out in dismay.

"It's a fake gun," Isy explained and hid the gun behind her back. "Don't panic. It only shoots **blanks**!"

"Where did you get it from?"

"I'll tell you later," promised Isy. They turned off the lights, locked the door to the recreation room and went upstairs to their room.

Amanda had only just slipped into bed when she asked Isy again about where she had got that 'terrible thing' from.

"In my bag at school," Isy told her. "Honest. Do you remember when Trischi said he was going to check all the bags just before the summer holidays? He said all he needed to do was to go through the classroom with a magnet to find all the knives, **knuckledusters** and air guns hidden in the bags. **Jelly Baby** must have slipped it into mine!"

"That sounds just like him!" fumed Amanda, who, like everybody else in the class, knew about

---

to shake – zittern; piece – Knarre;
blank (cartridge) – Platzpatrone; knuckleduster – Schlagring;
jelly baby – Gummibärchen

Hagen Golz's liking for jelly babies and weapons of all shapes and sizes. Then she yawned loudly. "Mama mia! What a night! Things like that don't even happen in Hollywood! Would you really have **pulled the trigger**?"

"Sure", said Isy. "I'd have shot him right between the eyes!"

They fell asleep giggling.

---

to pull the trigger – abdrücken, schießen

— 6 —

The next morning they went into the village.

They needed bread and butter, sausages and cheese, noodles, ketchup, stamps, canned food and nail polish. Amanda, whose cosmetics bag was almost bursting, had forgotten her favourite **nail polish**.

To begin with they stopped by the baker's. They'd got out of bed later than expected, and the first round of fresh rolls had landed on other people's breakfast tables. While Amanda started a cosy little chat with the baker's wife, Isy hungrily eyed up the **goods** on offer. It was warm in the small shop and it smelled great. As far as Isy could make out, the selection on offer consisted mainly of Danish pastries and cakes coated with masses of almonds, **poppy seeds** or fruit. Isy decided to spoil herself and Amanda with some crumble cake. Amanda was also the generous type and would often buy Isy a hot dog or an ice cream at the Italian. She also always **shared** the samples of soap,

---

nail polish – Nagellack; goods – Waren; poppy seed – Mohn; to share – teilen

shower gel and crème that she **cadged** from her Avon-mother. Isy looked impatiently at the clock over the empty bread baskets. How much longer was it going to take?

In the meantime the baker's wife had found out they were staying at the school lodge. It was good news to her, because her bakery always **supplied** the Berlin school kids with bread and rolls. She also knew that the lady in charge of the lodge key, Mrs King from 104 High Street, was attending a **silver wedding anniversary** in Kassel at the time. And most of all the baker's wife knew perfectly well that her son, that Ruky boy, was a **good-for-nothing**.

"He's got too much foreign blood in him. His father's Cuban!" she claimed and looked out of the corner of her eyes to see if anyone in the shop disagreed with her. But the two other customers, who were also waiting for bread, were deep in conversation.

"If my daughter ended up coming home with him!" sighed the baker's wife and rolled her eyes. Then she thrust her pasty face over the counter to the girls. "Keep well away from him!" she said in a **conspiratorial** voice. "He's already a criminal at the age of fourteen. Last year he grew hashish in the school garden. Fortunately the teachers spotted it in time!"

---

to cadge – abstauben; to supply – beliefern; silver wedding anniversary – Silberhochzeit; good-for-nothing – Taugenichts; conspiratorial – verschwörerisch

"He grew hashish in the school garden?" whispered Amanda. "**Far out**!"

"Too right! Far too far!" affirmed the baker's wife, but just then the assistant brought the fresh rolls out of the rear room and the **buxom** blonde lady was called into action.

As soon as they left the shop Isy **gave vent to her anger**. "I'm not buying anything there again! She's got a problem with foreigners!"

"But the crumble cake is tasty," said Amanda, taking another bite. "Do you believe that story about hash in the school garden?"

Isy shrugged her shoulders. "Sounds pretty stupid of him considering he's got his own garden at home..."

For a while they strolled up the High Street munching their cake. It was busier that morning than when they'd arrived the day before. Cars sped past, bicycles rang their bells, and loads of young mothers dragged their wild children home.

They went to the small supermarket and did the rest of their shopping. The only thing they didn't manage to buy was Amanda's nail polish. The range of colours on offer in the supermarket weren't loud enough. On their way back Isy suddenly stopped in front of the **butcher's**. A medium-sized, grey dog was sitting next to three steps leading up to the

---

Far out! – Wahnsinn!; buxom – drall;
to give vent to one's anger – seinem Ärger Luft machen;
butcher – Metzger

shop door. The dog started **wagging its** short **tail** on seeing her.

"I know him. That's Alfredo!" she said to Amanda and crouched down next to the dog. "So? How are you doing?" Isy asked him cheerfully, tickling his ears.

Amanda looked at Alfredo as if he were a ghost. "Are you sure you know him?"

"Sure! We met yesterday in the train. Isn't that right, Alfredo? You see, he's wagging his tail!" Isy **beamed** as if she'd just pulled off a magic trick.

As soon as they got back to the lodge they made a plan to clean the house. That was, after all, why they were in Green Meadows in the first place.

Isy suggested they clean the hallway first and then the windows. So they started clearing up all the rubbish left from the decorating, carrying the ladders and still usable pots of paint down to a **store-room** in the cellar, and set about cleaning the bedroom windows. Amanda wanted to throw in the towel as soon as she'd finished cleaning the first window.

"You call this a holiday?" she **scoffed** dramatically and rubbed the white spots of paint off the glass with a squeak. "The school should give us a medal for this."

Isy had to laugh. What was Amanda thinking of? "A medal? For what?"

---

to wag its tail – mit dem Schwanz wedeln; to beam – strahlen; storeroom – Lagerraum; to scoff – schnaufen

"For **slaving away** here of course! Or don't you call this slaving away while everybody else is sitting on their backside?"

"But nobody knows we're here!" Isy pointed out, cleaning her side of the window energetically. Now the world looked quite different. The trees in the garden were within reach all of a sudden.

"That's true, nobody would think we were that stupid," her friend agreed. "But it's still a shame no one can see how amazing we are!"

By the time the windows on the top floor were sparkling clean, Amanda was utterly **exhausted**. She **skulked** into the kitchen while Isy went down to the cellar to put more coal in the boiler. She now had the heating fully under control. She knew she'd only have to fill up the boiler one more time later in the evening to keep the house warm until the next morning.

Just as she was leaving the cellar, she remembered having seen a beautiful, old secretaire in the storeroom earlier as she'd brought down the things from the hallway. It was next to a pile of gardening tools and had clearly been abandoned by its **owner**. Perhaps it was damaged or had **woodworm**. In any case, Isy felt a sneaking curiosity overcoming her. Those old secretaires always had a **secret compartment**, didn't they? Isy had often seen old films in

---

to slave away – schuften; exhausted – erschöpft; to skulk – schleichen; owner – Besitzer; woodworm – Holzwurm; secret compartment – Geheimfach

which the distressed heroine or hero suddenly discovers a secret compartment in some dusty old piece of furniture in the attic, bringing to light the precious **family jewels** which had long been missing, or the **last will**, or a bundle of love letters bound by a faded, pale blue, silk ribbon.

She opened the squeaky door to the storeroom resolutely and went up to the old secretaire.

It didn't look very mysterious at all. Just dusty and a little forgotten.

She carefully opened the **lid**, which unfolded as a writing surface, and was disappointed to see that the interior seemed to offer only open secrets. Its four drawers were **warped** from the damp and full of worm holes.

In one of them Isy found a dead spider. The other three were empty. Nothing but dust and a few grains of sand. Presumably you could only ever find those fantastic secret compartments in the movies and in books, certainly not in reality. Just as Isy was about to close the lid in disappointment, she felt a **snag**. Something was **jamming**. It seemed to be part of the frontage, made of a fine grained, honey-coloured wood which connected the drawers and which she initially thought was the moulding. Only when she looked more closely could she see that it was a skilfully inserted **drawer**, the upper

---

family jewels – Familienschmuck; last will – Testament;
lid – Deckel; warped – verzogen; snag – Widerstand, Haken;
to jam – klemmen; drawer – Schublade

right corner of which hadn't been pushed back in precisely enough. Was this act of **carelessness** really about to help her discover a secret compartment? Isy could feel her heart pounding. Just then Amanda put her head around the cellar door.

"Iiiisssyyy! The spaghetti's *al dente*!"

Whatever that was supposed to mean.

"Coming!" called Isy.

Then she started tugging and pulling carefully at the supposed moulding, until millimetre by millimetre the drawer came out. Eventually she made it! Breathless with excitement she opened the drawer.

Her greatest fear – that it would be empty – turned out not to be the case, fortunately. Her slender hope, however – to uncover some wonderful secret from long forgotten times – also failed to **materialise**. But goodness knows what a shopping bag was doing in a place like this! Isy stared dumbfounded at her discovery.

She picked up the bag by the tips of her fingers. Its contents felt quite soft. She **wasn't** actually too **keen on** the idea of looking inside. What was she likely to find? Old **rags**? A discarded pullover which no one wanted to have any more? Or woollen leftovers from someone who'd long been knitting in heaven? When Isy finally decided to take a look into

---

carelessness – Unachtsamkeit; to materialise – sich verwirklichen; rag – Lumpen; to be keen on sth – etwas unbedingt wollen

the bag, she whistled between her teeth in surprise. Well what about that! Amanda would be amazed!

But Amanda was in a bad mood by the time Isy finally came into the kitchen. **In a huff** she dumped two portions of steaming spaghetti onto two plates and decorated them with a squirt of red ketchup.

"Didn't you hear me calling to say the spaghetti was *al dente*? They're all **sludgy** now!"

Isy thought the noodles looked perfectly normal, not at all sludgy. Besides, she had no idea what those mysterious words 'al dente' actually meant.

"Amanda," said Isy, trying to breathe as calmly as possible. "Your spaghetti's quite all right, but guess what I found in the cellar!"

"The bars of gold, of course!" scoffed Amanda.

"Wrong!" triumphed Isy. "The magic cap of invisibility! What do you say to that?"

---

to be in a huff – eingeschnappt sein; sludgy – matschig

— 7 —

"Bon appétit!" said Amanda, digging in to her noodles. When she was hungry, she had little patience for Isy's fun and games.

"You don't believe me, do you?" Isy put the shopping bag down provocatively in front of Amanda's plate. "I found it in a secret compartment in the old secretaire. The one in the storeroom. Go on, look inside!"

Amanda peeked into the bag and was **unimpressed**. "A woolly hat? So what?"

"What do you mean, 'so what'? You're sharp! Someone cut out holes for the eyes. Don't you get it?"

"Oh, man! Are you seeing ghosts again?"

"I don't need to see ghosts to smell that **something's rotten** here. It's as clear as daylight! This thing's a mask!"

"Then something must be wrong with your nose! Whenever you 'smell' something, it always ends up in a complete disaster. Why do you think

---

unimpressed – unbeeindruckt;
something is rotten – etw. ist faul

the others in the class call us the **'calamity** queens'?"

That was below the belt. Isy promptly lost her appetite. Amanda could be so cruel at times, bringing up those old stories again. Which one was she referring to now? Maybe the time with that funny little troll? He was about to dump his garbage bags in the park behind the school when she, Benedikt and Amanda **tied him up** to his own **steering-wheel**. The police were quick to identify the man: he wasn't some environmental exterminator, but the chairman of a citizen's initiative to 'Keep Our Parks Clean'. All he was trying to do was draw attention to **contamination** in parks. The least Isy could do was apologise to him afterwards. She also gave him a new pack of blue garbage bags.

Or was Amanda referring to the little **mishap** with the dead mushroom picker? Isy had discovered his fresh **corpse** underneath an old **spruce** during a class trip to the Schorfheide. Only he ended up being not quite as dead as she thought. When the Murder Squad finally located the spot which she'd so precisely described to them, the corpse had woken up from its midday nap and was energetically picking mushrooms in the nearby pine forest.

If her reputation really was that bad, then Amanda had to carry at least 50% of the responsi-

---

calamity – Katastrophe; to tie sb up – fesseln; steering-wheel – Lenkrad; contamination – Verschmutzung; mishap – Unglück; corpse – Leiche; spruce – Fichte

bility. Twenty-five per cent for the deadly egg salad which she'd made for Isy's birthday party: instead of dressing it with a tartar sauce, Amanda had smeared the eggs with her Avon-mother's favourite beauty mask which had been lying in the same drawer in the fridge. After this slight error of judgement, Saskia, Sophie and Binette were sick for two days. Jennifer Niemann, who was stuck on the toilet for half a week and got a terrible **rash**, came up with the theory that Amanda wanted to get her out of the way because she'd been chairwoman of the Young Pioneers in her class back in the **GDR**. That's what you call a class struggle!

Amanda's remaining 25% share of the "calamity queens" reputation was due to a class trip which she'd organised to make some extra pocket money. Instead of working as **extras** on the set of an adventure movie in the famous Babelsberg studios, the class ended up in an overripe field of tomatoes near the town of Werder. Amanda had inadvertently led them onto the wrong bus. Although the farmers were delighted that they'd come to help with the harvest, and they ended up earning the same amount of money, a few girls had been expecting to be discovered as tomorrow's stars and still hadn't forgiven Amanda to this day.

"You can't talk!" countered Isy. "All I have to say is 'Potsdam bus station'!"

---

rash – Ausschlag; GDR/German Democratic Republic – DDR; extra – Statist

Amanda, who was just twirling her last noodle onto her fork, turned as red as **beetroot**. Isy couldn't help thinking about how they'd rushed out of the main station in such hurry because the train from Berlin had arrived so late. No wonder they'd ended up on the wrong bus!

"It wouldn't have happened if the trains here in your beloved East weren't as slow as snails!" she argued feebly.

"Our East is now your West. And besides, it was one of *your* trains."

"No quality train can run properly on *your* **lousy tracks**!"

"Our lousy tracks are now your lousy tracks, too," corrected Isy unmoved. "We're one nation now, dearest Amanda."

Amanda tapped a finger against her forehead and cleared away the plates without saying a word. Usually at the end of a silly dispute like this they ended up **laughing their heads off**. But this time neither of them gave in. Their stinging reproaches seemed to have dug too deep.

Isy snatched up the shopping list from the table. "So you're not coming with me to the police?"

"Do you want to make us look ridiculous?"

"A **piece of evidence** is never ridiculous!"

"Evidence of what?"

---

beetroot – Rote Bete; lousy – beschissen; tracks – Schienen; to laugh one's head off – sich kaputt lachen; piece of evidence – Beweisstück

"Of whatever! A bank robbery! Kidnapping! A raid on the supermarket! Breaking and entering into a branch of the Savings Bank...!"

"You read too many thrillers!"

"And you read too few!"

After this conversation, Isy threw on her parka and went out into the garden. She didn't care what Amanda did. Sometimes Isy had no idea why she was friends with her! It was quiet and still a bit damp in the lodge's garden. A fine, barely visible **fog** was hanging in the cool air. Isy hadn't seen the garden in daylight, and she started looking around curiously. She spotted a dried-out **pond**, a deserted barbecue surrounded by a few tree stumps serving as seats, and an old rose bush with hundreds of berries on its bare branches, glowing like tiny autumn fires.

Just as she was about to pluck one of the soft fruits she spotted a **cinnamon-coloured** bird the size of a **pigeon**. It was perched in the oak tree and its wings were adorned with shiny blue feathers. What was that? An exotic bird **gone astray**?

"Hey, say something", urged Isy, but the bird just looked at her haughtily with its clever eyes.

Eventually the cinnamon-coloured stranger flew off and headed towards the forest. "Ra, ra, ra", it screeched three times, but it sounded more like, "na-na, na-na-na!"

---

fog – Nebel; pond – Teich; cinnamon-coloured – zimtfarben; pigeon – Taube; to go astray – sich verirren

Amanda had opened the window and was shouting at the top of her voice: Isy's parents had called, wanting to know how they were getting on.

"I told them it's all under control here!" Amanda leant out of the window expectantly. "Did you hear me?"

"Yeah, I heard!" said Isy from the berry bush.

"They said hello. You should call them back sometime."

Amanda slammed the window noisily. At least they were talking again. Oh, that Amanda with her favourite saying, 'completely bananas'!

The boys in the class had called her '**grilled sausage**' as soon as she had drifted into Year Four from Nuremberg, although she was born in West Berlin before the Wall. The girls eyed the "West Import" with cool curiosity for the first year after **reunification**. Jennifer Niemann, who was particularly bothered by Amanda's trendy clothes, even claimed that the New Girl from the former West couldn't possibly be intelligent, because it was a fact that German, History and Natural Sciences had always been badly taught over there. As Amanda had none of these subjects in her **timetable** apart from German, the claim was never **confirmed**. On the other hand she amazed her classmates with her good computer skills. She talked freely and wasn't

---

grilled sausage – Rostbratwurst;
reunification – Wiedervereinigung; timetable – Stundenplan;
confirmed – bestätigt

at all shy, and whenever a lesson was too boring, she took out her **knitting** and **infuriated** all the teachers. Trischi once let Amanda spend a whole hour clattering away with her needles until she got bored of that, too. Then he asked her to knit him a winter pullover with a **herringbone pattern** in his favourite colour. When Amanda bashfully admitted that she couldn't knit herringbone, he reacted as if he were upset. Then he asked her not to take out her needles in his lesson until she'd learned how to knit herringbone. As far as Isy could remember, Amanda never knitted in a lesson after that. In comparison to other disturbances, the teachers had to **admit** that Amanda's carefree knitting was no more than a harmless provocation. Ever since Jelly Baby had fired a blank in the middle of the Peasant's Revolt and a few incognitos had started a fire in the corridor to **stall** a music test, it was clear that the signs of these violent times were not going to pass by Year Six **without a trace**.

"Ra!" screeched the cinnamon-coloured bird again, somewhere nearby in the forest. Isy decided to go back into the house. It was slowly getting dark. She thought again about the woolly hat with the cut-out eyeholes. She'd take it around to the police station the next day.

With or without Amanda.

---

knitting – Strickzeug; to infuriate – rasend machen;
to admit – zugeben; herringbone pattern – Fischgrätenmuster;
to stall sth – etw. aufhalten; without a trace – spurlos

— 8 —

That night Isy dreamed about the cinnamon-coloured bird. He was **perched** on her **blanket** and asked her if she wanted to fly back home with him.

"Your home, where is it?" asked Isy inquisitively.

"Schurpurmadraskeninkongheli," answered the bird with dignity.

"Where on earth is that?" asked Isy, never having heard of this strange country before, when suddenly a door creaked in her dream.

Slightly **dazed** she woke up and sat upright. It was still the middle of the night. Amanda was **snoring** quietly in the top bunk bed. Had Isy just dreamed that a door had squeaked, or was a door really creaking somewhere in the house?

At the same time Isy realised she could only wake up Amanda if and when she was quite sure that something was wrong in the house. After all, the **disgrace** with the hedgehog from last night was still fresh in her memory.

---

to perch – sitzen; blanket – Bettdecke; dazed – benommen;
to snore – schnarchen; disgrace – Blamage

She listened to the darkness until somewhere in the house a door began to creak again. It could only be in the cellar – probably the door to the storeroom. Isy jumped to her feet in a flash and shook Amanda awake.

"Amanda, wake up! There's someone in the cellar!"

"Not this again!" moaned Amanda sleepily and buried her face into her pillow. "It'll be that hedgehog again. Let me sleep!"

"But a hedgehog can't make a door in the cellar squeak!"

"Sure he can," mumbled Amanda. "He can cough, too." Then she took a deep sigh and fell silent. No question, she was fast asleep again.

Isy was annoyed about Amanda and **felt her way** into the corridor alone. Some friend! Snoring in bed while she had to defend the house! She carefully felt out the first step of the staircase. If this was going to happen every night, she'd soon be a specialist in night-time staircases. Just then Isy thought she could hear soft footsteps. Horrified, she **froze to the spot** and stared down into the dark hallway. Was she seeing things or did somebody just **scurry** past the stairs to the front door? It was difficult to see, because the light from the street lamp was very faint. By the time Isy started to scream, the ghost had already passed.

---

to feel one's way – sich vortasten; to freeze to the spot – wie angewurzelt stehen bleiben; to scurry – huschen

"Isy, what's up?" called Amanda from somewhere in the darkness. Her voice was shrill with fear.

"Somebody just ran through the hallway!" panted Isy. "Go on, turn the lights on, Amanda!"

The light flickered on over the staircase, and Isy saw her friend in her long, yellow **nightie** trembling with fear on the top step. "Did you really see someone?"

"Just for a second. Then he ran out of the front door."

"The front door?" asked Amanda in disbelief.

"Yeah. For sure! Come on, let's take a look."

Amanda followed Isy hesitantly into the hallway. Together they took a closer look at the front door. How strange! It was closed! And not only that, it was locked, too. Isy could feel Amanda looking at her critically.

"He must have a key," Isy concluded. "I didn't hear him coming in, either. If the door to the storeroom hadn't squeaked so loudly, I'd still be asleep."

"Me, too," said Amanda emphatically and yawned.

Could it be that Amanda didn't believe her? That she **doubted** Isy's word?

"I'll prove it!" said Isy **doggedly** and dragged Amanda down to the cellar. As she expected, the door to the storeroom squeaked terribly loud. It was

---

nightie – Nachthemd; to doubt – bezweifeln;
doggedly – hartnäckig, entschlossen

precisely the sound she'd heard twice. **Unerring,** Isy headed to the old secretaire. Someone had **tampered with** the lid. Thanks to his **haste**, the intruder hadn't closed the secretaire properly.

Isy showed Amanda the tiny corner of the secret compartment which hadn't been slotted back precisely into the frontage.

"And are you quite sure you closed it properly at lunchtime?"

"Do you think I'm gaga or what?"

For a moment everything was very still in the cellar. Only the pipes, in which the heat was beginning to **recede**, cracked a little. That was physics. The law of expansion. The metal was now contracting again. Benedikt had had to do a test about it a few weeks ago. Isy could feel she was beginning to shiver from the cold.

"So you think I'm out of my mind?"

Embarrassed, Amanda **squirmed** like a worm.

"N-n-n-no. But you have to admit, people do get things **muddled up**. Especially when they're as imaginative as you."

"I'm not as imaginative as you think!"

"Of course you are. Sometimes you admit it, sometimes you don't. Whichever suits you best."

"Alright then, but what are you trying to tell me?"

---

unerring – zielsicher; to tamper with – sich an etw. zu schaffen machen; haste – Eile; to recede – nachlassen; to squirm – sich winden; to muddle up – etwas durcheinander bringen

"My mother always imagines everything as well. Last year in Tunisia, for instance. We were at a salt lake and all of a sudden she said she could see a motorway with cars bombing over it."

"And why shouldn't she have seen a motorway?" asked Isy.

"Because there wasn't one. Just desert. As far as the eye could see. And the only means of transport were our camels." Amanda took a deep breath. "My dad said she had a Fata Morgana."

Amanda shook her head without saying a word.

And she was a **coward**, too! That hurt Isy. She slotted the secret compartment back into the frontage and closed the lid. Then she went to bed without looking at her friend again.

But she couldn't sleep. Amanda also tossed and turned on her mattress, and the **bedstead** creaked. In the end she couldn't bear the **standoff** any longer.

"Alright then," said Amanda. "Let's presume that someone really was in the house. He probably wanted to nick something worthwhile, not just some old **bobble hat**. Don't you think?"

"Depends how much it's worth to him. And the fact that he went back to the secret compartment to get it, is proof that it must be very **valuable** to him. Either it's his woolly hat and he wants to get rid of it because it can be used against him, or it doesn't

---

coward – Feigling; bedstead – Bettgestell; standoff – Distanz, Schweigen; bobble hat – Pudelmütze; valuable – wertvoll

belong to him and he wants to get a **reward** for it. That's logical, isn't it?"

Instead of replying Amanda yawned loudly.

"Anyway, at least we can sleep in peace now. Whether you're right or not, he's got his hat back now, and he won't be coming back again."

"I wouldn't be so sure of that."

"Why not?"

"Because he can't have found the woolly hat!"

"But you just said it was in the secret compartment!"

"Was, Amanda, *was* in the secret compartment. But I didn't put it back. I hid it. Very well in fact. You'll never guess where it is!"

"Really?"

"Really."

"Okay, then tell me!" Amanda didn't seem to want to waste time guessing.

"Do you promise you won't be angry?"

"I promise!"

"It's under your pillow. Good night!"

---

reward – Belohnung

— 9 —

The next day the weather had changed. The calm October days seemed to be over. A wind had whipped up in the early morning and grown into a boisterous storm which was now whistling around the house. The **birches bent** under its will. It swept the leaves off the beech trees, whistled into the chimney and made the old roof **groan**. Isy and Amanda took their time over breakfast. Cleaning the windows wouldn't be possible during a hurricane like this anyway.

While they enjoyed their food, they worked out where the best **hiding place** would be for the woolly hat. Amanda had no intention of spending another night sleeping on top of a piece of criminal evidence. By the time they'd finished their breakfast, they'd had a number of good ideas: in the pantry, behind the bookshelf, next to the **fuse box** in the cellar, under the bathtub in the washroom, in the **cistern** of the girls' toilet, in the deep freeze com-

---

birch – Birke; to bend – sich biegen; to groan – ächzen;
hiding place – Versteck; fuse box – Sicherungskasten;
cistern – Spülkasten

partment of the refrigerator. They liked the last idea most of all.

They took the black bobble hat out of the bedroom, put it in a metal **bowl** and buried it in the slithery spaghetti left over from the previous day. Then they put the bowl into the deep freeze and turned the temperature as low as possible.

"Voilà," said Amanda. "Spaghetti criminale." Then they started to clean the floor.

Amanda turned on their cassette recorder. While they scratched off the **daubs of paint** splattered over the amber-coloured floorboards in the hallway with kitchen knives, they sang along to all the songs they knew. Then they washed the floor with brushes. They always liked singing together, though other people didn't always find it so good. Like in the quiet corner of an **ice cream parlour**, or on the bus, or once even in a gallery. The girls could never understand why other people weren't just pleased to see such happy people instead of telling them off angrily. But most of the time it didn't bother them. Most of the time they just sang a bit quieter.

They were singing 'Hot time, summer in the city' when all of a sudden the phone in the hallway started to ring. It was a shrill sound and completely unexpected. The girls were so **startled** that Amanda dropped the knife before hurrying over to

---

bowl – Schüssel; daub of paint – Farbklecks; ice cream parlour – Eiscafé; startled – erschrocken

the telephone. Isy heard her talking to someone, but she couldn't make out what it was about. If the call had been for her, then Amanda would already have told her so.

Who would have thought that she'd end up here in Green Meadows scrubbing floors with an uncomplicated, hard-working Amanda? Not her, and not Amanda either. She really was a true friend!

The first time she'd seen Amanda, Isy would never have thought her best friend was capable of doing anything like this. They'd first met at school. Amanda had sat down at the desk in front of her wearing a raspberry-coloured jumpsuit and looking like a portion of **stewed** fruit. The hand which the new girl held out to her was adorned with six silver rings. Isy spent the next few weeks checking out the happy-go-lucky West Import with a certain **reserve**. She let Amanda know she shouldn't **get big-headed** just because she came from Nuremberg.

The friendship between her and Amanda began in that dark hour of the Gulf War. They were bombarded by horrific round-the-clock images on TV: Kuwait **ablaze** and people cowering in their cellars with gas masks over their frightened faces in faraway Israel.

They saw little old mothers, babies and even a girl, all with gas masks on. The girl looked like she

---

to stew – einkochen; reserve – Zurückhaltung;
to get big-headed – eingebildet werden; ablaze – in Flammen

was the same age as them and she'd taken her dog into the cellar to protect it. The black mongrel, who, of course, couldn't wear a gas mask, squatted in a plastic **oxygen tent** to survive the possible poison gas attack. Sirens rang out over the city. Everybody, including the girl with the dog, **was scared out of their wits**.

Isy and Amanda were also scared. They were a long way away from the scenes of war, safe and sound in Amanda's parents' flat in Berlin. But at one point there was a big **close-up** of the dog and the girl's frightened face, and Amanda began to **sob** miserably. Isy also had a **lump** in her throat. The girl in Israel was probably the same age as her!

After they'd seen this news report, they decided to join together and do something against the war. Isy wrote a letter to the girl with the black dog and pinned it on the class noticeboard. Underneath the letter Amanda did a picture of the mongrel in its oxygen tent.

The article went down well, although Jennifer Niemann pointed out that the Israelis had also done their bit to annoy the Arabs.

That was two years ago, and since then there had been so many other wars in the world that Amanda and Isy would have had their work cut out to fill the noticeboard against each of them. It was,

---

oxygen tent – Sauerstoffzelt; to be scared out of one's wit – zu Tode erschrocken sein; close-up – Nahaufnahme; to sob – schluchzen; lump – Kloß

as her father said with a shake of his head every day after the news, as if the world had gone mad! A fine mess if one considered that Amanda and she weren't even thirteen yet…

"It was the post office!" called Amanda and came running up the stairs. "They've got a packet for us!"

"A packet?" asked Isy in disbelief. "For who?"

"Well, for you or me, I guess. I didn't ask them who exactly. Anyway, we can pick it up until midday, or it will come tomorrow with the postal van."

"Amanda", said Isy, frowning anxiously. "There's something funny going on here! Why would anyone send us a packet? No one knows we're here!"

"Our parents know."

"True, our parents do, but why would they send us a packet? Or is it your birthday?"

"Okay, make it all sound much more complicated than it really is!" sighed Amanda, annoyed. "I presume you're thinking about Mr Mysterious from last night."

"Exactly."

"And you reckon he's sent us a letter bomb or something?"

Amanda had tried to sound serious and believable, but by the time she'd finished, Isy noticed she was almost bursting with laughter.

"Go ahead, **take the mickey**," said Isy with dig-

---

to take the mickey – sich lustig machen

nity. "You won't find anything about tricks like these in your royal reports."

"What tricks?"

"Like the trick to get someone out of their house so they can **search** the place."

"But they said it was the German Post Office!"

"Anyone can say that!" Isy's voice had a touch of **scorn**. "And you're exactly the kind of person who would fall for something like that."

"Then you answer the telephone next time!" shouted Amanda furiously. "You still haven't said what you think we should do. The post office is going to close in an hour!"

Isy thought about the situation for a second.

"What about if one of us stays here to **guard** the house?"

"Bad idea!" said Amanda decisively. "You said we were going to do everything together, so let's do it."

---

to search – durchsuchen; scorn – Verachtung;
to guard – bewachen

— 10 —

The post office was on the other side of the village. On their way there, the autumn storm tugged grimly at the girls' clothes and blew leaves into their faces.

When they finally managed to escape the storm and went into the front room of the post office, they realised that they were almost the only **customers**. There was just one other person standing at the parcels counter. He had turned up the collar of his trench coat and was wearing a brown **beret** over his thin hair. Isy recognised him **straightaway** nonetheless. Thrilled, she nudged Amanda. "Hey, I know him!"

Instead of answering, her friend blew her nose noisily. She'd had enough of Isy's wild imaginings.

"I really do know him," Isy assured her quietly. "That's the owner of Alfredo, the dog we saw yesterday in front of the butcher's!"

Just then a post office **employee** heaved a medium-sized box onto the counter.

---

customer – Kunde; beret – Baskenmütze;
straightaway – sofort, auf der Stelle; employee – Angestellte

"That could sink a battleship!" she puffed. "Is it your new book, Mr Rimpau?"

"Yes, the new thriller!" confirmed the customer and signed for the packet in a book which the lady pushed towards him. "As soon as I've unpacked it, you'll get your copy as usual, Mrs Lilli!"

"But a signed one, I hope!" beamed the post office lady.

Isy's heart missed a beat as well. So he was called Mr Rimpau? And he wrote thrillers, too. It was great, the people she knew!

She waited **on tenterhooks** for Mr Rimpau to turn around and recognise her. If need be, she would have to remind him that they'd met on the train. But that wasn't the case. As soon as Alfredo's master turned around to make for the door with his packet of books, he stopped in his tracks.

"Oh, Alfredo's new friend! What are you doing in this beautiful place?"

"Er, we're just staying at the school lodge," explained Isy and introduced him to Amanda. She **briefly** explained what she and Amanda were doing in Green Meadows. After thinking about it **for a split second**, she decided not to mention all the disturbing **incidents**. "We'll have the house cleaned up by tomorrow at the latest. Then it's holiday time!" and with that, she ended her report.

Behind the parcels counter Mrs Lilli began to

---

on tenterhooks – gespannt; briefly – kurz; for a split second – für den Bruchteil einer Sekunde; incident – Zwischenfall

rattle her enormous key ring. Mr Rimpau looked at his watch. "The post office is preparing for lunch, ladies! If you want, I can **give** you **a lift** back to the lodge. I'm passing by there anyway."

That was an offer they couldn't **refuse**! While Mr Rimpau carried his books to the car, the post office lady handed Isy a parcel over the counter. Isy stared at the packet with her name on it. The sender's name and address were in the top left-hand corner: Olaf Schütze. Isy immediately knew what her dad had sent her: the camera she'd left behind!

She hastily signed in Mrs Lilli's big book, carefully avoiding making eye contact with Amanda, who was staring at her **derisively**. **Don't mock the afflicted**, she thought! The writer was waiting for them in his burgundy Golf. Inside there was a warm smell of leather, petrol and tobacco. This time the autumn storm blew the leaves against Mr Rimpau's windscreen rather than into their faces.

Isy told him that she'd seen Alfredo in front of the butcher's the day before. "He recognised me straightaway!" she said proudly. Amanda was amazed how familiar Isy was with Mr Rimpau, and Isy enjoyed rubbing it in. Though not for very long. Her best friend started asking Mr Rimpau a whole stream of questions from the back seat and within no time had hijacked the conversation.

---

to give sb a lift – jmd. mitnehmen; to refuse – ablehnen; derisively – spöttisch; Don't mock the afflicted! – Wer den Schaden hat, braucht für den Spott nicht zu sorgen!

First of all she wanted to know if a writer needed to have a lot of imagination. Then she asked if too much imagination could be bad for one's health.

As an example she told Mr Rimpau about a friend of hers, whose name she didn't want to **mention**, who always thought there was a mystery behind everything. She saw ghosts everywhere, and even when she had to pick up a perfectly normal packet from the post office, she suspected it was a nasty trick by some mysterious stranger who was trying to get her out of her house.

Isy could feel the blood rushing into her face. Was Amanda **off her rocker**? Did she want to disgrace her to death in front of Mr Rimpau?

"Can you stop, please!? I want to get out!" she said to the writer before he could respond to Amanda's questions. Taken aback, Mr Rimpau put his foot down on the **brakes**.

"I sometimes get car sick!" she excused herself. "We can walk the last bit, can't we, Amanda?"

She thanked Mr Rimpau for the lift. Then Isy had one of her bright ideas. She **plucked up courage** and asked Mr Rimpau if he'd like to do a reading for Year Six in the school lodge next week. The class would just love it.

"Oh, yes, please!" implored Amanda. "We've never had a real writer as a guest!"

---

to mention – erwähnen; off one's rocker – übergeschnappt; brake – Bremse; to pluck up courage – den Mut zusammennehmen

"Then you can tell us how you get all your ideas in this peaceful place!" suggested Isy.

The writer thanked them for the invitation, promised to give them a call at the lodge to make a date, and added in an anxious tone of voice that Green Meadows was no longer such a peaceful place. A robbery at the post office less than two weeks ago had awakened it from its rosy sleep.

"A robbery with a mask?" asked Isy as quick as a flash. She could feel her heart pounding against her ribs.

"Someone with a black woolly hat. At least, that's what Lilli said, and she should know. She was on duty at the time. But it was in the papers, too."

Then Mr Rimpau said they shouldn't hesitate to give him a call at his weekend house in the neighbouring village of Bollwitz in the case of flooding, a **power cut** or a forest fire. Then he drove off with a beep of his **horn**.

"Since when do you get car sick?" asked Amanda furiously.

"Since today."

"Oh, yeah. From what?"

"From your **gabbing**! Don't you think I guessed who you were talking about with your 'funny friend'?"

"So what? I'm worried about you."

"Because I see 'ghosts'?"

---

power cut – Stromausfall; horn – Hupe;
gabbing – Gequatsche

"Maybe."

"Then I'm afraid I'm going to have to disappoint you. I don't see ghosts at all! If you'd been listening properly, then you wouldn't have missed the fact that the post office was robbed two weeks ago by someone wearing a black woolly hat! I hope **the penny has** finally **dropped** in your thick skull!"

"Are you starting with all that again?" hissed Amanda. "Forget that stupid woolly hat. Wasn't the fiasco in the post office enough for you?" She glanced scornfully at the packet which Isy was carrying under her arm. "So much for 'someone wants to get us out of the house so they can search the place!' A perfectly normal packet! And the Mr Mysterious is none other than your dad. But I guess the perfectly normal isn't crazy enough for you!"

By the time Amanda had finished, they'd arrived back at the lodge, and Amanda dashed into the front garden. Isy had trouble keeping up with her. She could only hear **shreds** of what Amanda was saying.

"... don't want to hear another word! ... just give it a break! ... load of rubbish! ... pack my things ... get out of here! Then you can ... clean the lodge with Mr Mysterious!"

For goodness sake, what had got into her?

---

the penny has dropped – der Groschen ist gefallen;
shred – Fetzen

Amanda Bornstein on the **warpath**! Concerned, Isy put down the parcel onto the heavy oak table in the hall. Behind her she could hear Amanda stamping up the stairs. Anybody could make a mistake! Far worse was the fact that Amanda refused to see all the obvious links. What else had to happen for her to finally grasp what was going on?

Isy hung up her parka in the cloakroom and was just about to put on her slippers when a shrill scream rang through the house. There was no question: it was Amanda.

The very next moment Amanda was standing at the top of the stairs as white as a sheet.

"Help! A burglar!" she stammered, horrified. "The whole room… someone's searched through all our things! I think I'm going to be sick!"

---

warpath – Kriegspfad

— 11 —

So she was right! And she'd known it all along! There was a slight trace of **satisfaction** in Isy's voice as she asked her friend: "Are you sure you didn't see a Fata Morgana, dearest Amanda?"

But the person at the top of the stairs was trembling so much that Isy decided to generously forgive Amanda and put aside her **vindictive ridicule**. At least Amanda would believe her more from now on.

"Is anything missing?" she asked quickly.

"No idea!" groaned Amanda. "I haven't got a clue about anything anymore!"

When Isy visited the scene of the crime on the top floor, she could see that Amanda hadn't been **exaggerating**. Mr Mysterious had done a good job. He'd turned everything upside down. Pillows and blankets were piled up messily, and the wardrobe and all the bags had been emptied recklessly onto the floor.

Dumbfounded, Isy climbed over the pile of un-

---

satisfaction – Befriedigung; vindictive ridicule – rachsüchtiger Spott; to exaggerate – übertreiben

derwear, pullovers, tapes, tissues and jeans, and fished a pink poetry album out of a pile of socks.

"What on earth did you bring all this with you for?!" she said. No wonder Amanda needed a personal **porter**!

Then she flopped down in the middle of the chaos.

"Let's think! What we need now is logic."

"**I'd rather** you told me how you knew someone was going to break in. And how come the call from the post office was still true? I just don't get it!"

"Because the two things didn't have anything to do with each other. Pure **coincidence**! But it does prove we were being watched."

"But by who? The guy from last night?"

"Exactly! He's still looking for his woolly hat. Or did he steal anything?"

Amanda shook her head without saying a word. She really **had the creeps**. The idea that someone was watching them gave her **goose-pimples**. And he'd even searched through her blue suitcase!

"Right, let's put one and one together!" Isy got to the point, a serious expression on her face. "He can't live far from here, because he was watching us when we left the house to go to the post office! What's more – and this is extremely important – he's got **access** to a key to the house, which means

---

porter – Kofferträger; I'd rather … – Mir wär's lieber …; coincidence – Zufall; to have the creeps – sich gruseln; goose-pimples – Gänsehaut; access – Zugang

he can come and go when he wants! Are you thinking what I'm thinking?"

"I can't believe this," said Amanda melancholically. "I can just imagine how great it would be on Gran Canaria right now. The sun beating down, me lying on the beach, having a swimming race with my dad. And in the evening I'd help myself to a generous portion from the cold buffet until my stomach almost burst." She giggled sadly.

"Fine, now get right back onto the plane to Green Meadows!" Isy suggested impatiently. "We're going to pay Mr Mysterious a visit!"

A few minutes later they were standing in front of the small house at Number 104 High Street. The wind had subsided a little by midday, but Amanda was annoyed that she'd left her scarf behind in the hallway because of Isy's rushed departure. That was typical of her. Or as her mother would say, she'd barely **recovered** and she was back to being Miss Careless again. But what on earth did Isy want at the Kings' house? She didn't actually think that arrogant boy Ruky was Mr Mysterious? Without **hesitating** Isy threw open the garden gate and marched straight up to the house.

"Shouldn't we ring first?" asked Amanda tentatively.

"No. Never lose the element of surprise!"

Isy didn't go up to the front door, but went around the veranda to the left of the house. There

---

to recover – sich erholen; to hesitate – zögern

were two large windows at the back, and in the garden was a neatly harvested **vegetable patch**. A huge pumpkin adorned the middle of the vegetable patch. In its barren, autumnal surroundings it shone like a fallen moon.

The first of the two windows was slightly **ajar**, and a familiar smell of fried eggs and bacon drifted out into the cool autumnal air. Amanda sniffed hungrily at the air.

"What are we doing here?" she whispered breathlessly. "Do you think it was him who robbed the post office?"

Instead of answering, Isy climbed up the wall of the house and **propped** herself **up** on the windowsill. She looked into the kitchen.

It was a very beautiful kitchen made of honey-coloured wood. There was a linen table mat and an empty plate on the round dining table. A knife and fork framed it neatly on either side. Isy was speechless. Did this guy really **make** such **a big deal** out of eating lunch alone? She was almost ashamed to think about how she always chaotically **wolfed down** her lunch when no one was at home. She was always in too much of a rush to even sit down.

She could only see the cook from behind. He was standing at the stove with his back to her, stirring something in a pan. This time he wasn't wear-

---

vegetable patch – Gemüsebeet; ajar – angelehnt, halb offen;
to prop up – abstützen; to make a big deal – Tamtam machen;
to wolf down – verschlingen/wegputzen

ing a red polo neck but a long, bright green herringbone pullover. It looked like the Queen had knitted it herself. Isy thought briefly about how embarrassing it would be if she'd **got the wrong end of the stick**, but then she took a deep breath and pushed open the window.

"Hey!" said Isy, trying to sound **laid-back**. "Smells good!"

If Ruky was startled by Isy's unexpected appearance at the kitchen window, he didn't show it at all.

"What do you want?" he drawled. He'd asked exactly the same question three days ago as they stood in front of his front door. Maybe it was his favourite question.

"We've got a lot to talk about!" Isy could feel her fingers going **numb** on the cold stone of the window sill. And she still hadn't found a proper support for her feet. Don't slip! Not now! "Like the two **break-ins** at the school lodge. One last night and one two hours ago while we were at the post office."

"There have been quite a few break-ins around here recently!" Ruky confirmed as cool as a coke on ice. Then he took the frying pan with the scrambled eggs off the hotplate. "You should go to the police!"

"Are you serious?"

"Sure."

---

to get the wrong end of the stick – etw. falsch verstehen; laid-back – locker; numb – taub; break-in – Einbruch

No, really, not a hint of shame! Not a trace of a **guilty conscience**! Was he really so **unscrupulous**, or was she miles off the mark with her suspicion?

Isy decided to risk a last, decisive strike.

"Good idea with the police!" she agreed **sanctimoniously**. "Why didn't we think of that? I mean, we found this old, black woolly hat the other day, and then we heard the post office was robbed recently. By someone with a woolly hat. I mean..."

There was a long silence in which she had no idea if she'd **hit the bull's-eye** or not. Ruky King poked around his scrambled egg on his plate and was as cool as if she'd just read him the **stock market rates** or the weather report from yesterday. Then he sat down at the table. Without turning around he called out: "Come in! The door's open!"

---

guilty conscience – schlechtes Gewissen;
unscrupulous – abgebrüht; sanctimoniously – scheinheilig;
to hit the bull's-eye – ins Schwarze treffen; stock market rate – Börsenkurs

— 12 —

There you go! Isy knew it all along. Just a bit of patience! Satisfied with her work, Isy slipped back down to the damp grass.

"We've got him!" she told her friend.

"Well go on, tell me!" urged Amanda. "Did he really rob the post office?"

"I don't think so. But he's definitely got something to do with the woolly hat!"

Then they went around the house and entered through the veranda. Mr Mysterious hadn't touched his food. It looked like he'd lost his appetite. Instead he'd lit a cigarette.

"And what about me?" asked Amanda. Ruky offered her a cigarette. What a **poser**! thought Isy. Pretending to be cool. Then they let Ruky do the talking. Within a few minutes they knew his story.

It was the story of a fanatical car lover who'd **succumbed** to his burning desire to drive a car on a number of occasions.

"It's pure freedom!" said Ruky, exhaling the smoke through his nose.

---

poser – Angeber; to succumb – nachgeben, erliegen

At first things went perfectly. He went for a **joy-ride** on three different nights, each time parking the car back in front of the owner's house without being noticed. Okay, with a **bust lock** and a bit less petrol in its tank, but otherwise intact.

But on his fourth dream ride around the dark country roads, the Seat's engine started **stuttering**. Just as he was looking for a can of petrol in the trunk, he saw a police car approaching. He dropped what he was doing and ran off into the nearby woods. He spent the night in a **raised hide**.

When he got home the next day, he knew he'd landed a **whammy** with the Seat. In his trouser pocket was the black woolly hat which the post office lady, Mrs Lilli, had described to the newspapers. He'd taken it out of the glove compartment, thinking it was a **cleaning rag**. He was going to wipe his hands on it after he'd filled up the tank.

The idea of hiding the valuable discovery in the old, abandoned secretaire in the school lodge seemed like a good idea to him until they turned up.

"And now?" blurted out Amanda. "Are you going to take the woolly hat to the police?"

"The police?" laughed Ruky scornfully. "I'd have to be pretty stupid! They'd do me for joy-riding. They call me the 'Seat **Nicker**'. It was always Seats."

---

joy-ride – Spritztour; bust lock – aufgebrochenes Schloss;
to stutter – stottern; raised hide – Hochsitz;
whammy – Volltreffer; cleaning rag – Putzlappen; nicker – Klauer

Well what a surprise! He even had a name with the police! Isy looked at Mrs King's razor-sharp son with a mixture of curiosity, astonishment and indignation.

"What if you'd have **run someone over** and killed them?"

"I wouldn't have run anyone over!" Ruky wriggled uneasily in his chair. Then he grinned broadly: "Honest!"

Isy reckoned he was as old as Benedikt. Year Eight, or twice in the Seventh. You never really knew. Compared to this guy, Benedikt was **as pure as snow**. But then again he wasn't nearly as good-looking. Ruky was wearing his long, shaggy hair open today. It hung down to his slim shoulders and made him look a bit more honest and vulnerable. Maybe he wasn't the tough guy he made himself out to be.

"Did you find out who the Seat **belonged to**?"

Isy felt his black eyes dart **to and fro**, bright and alert. That's good. He should know he wasn't dealing with an idiot. She could do a lot more than **put two and two together**.

"Let's just say, I'm close."

"Our room looks like a pigsty, by the way!" Amanda chipped in. During the entire conversation

---

to run sb over – jmd. überfahren; as pure as snow – lammfromm;
to belong to sb – jmd. gehören; to and fro – hin und her;
to put two and two together – logisch denken;
to chip in – sich einmischen

she'd been staring at Ruky's scrambled eggs as if she were hypnotised. "Is there anything you'd like to say to *that*?"

"Sure." Ruky just wouldn't give up playing the cool guy. "Which of you two travelled here with the **shooter**?"

"Isolde," said Amanda giggling. "But it's just a **dummy**."

"It's not a dummy!" contradicted Isy. "Jelly Baby shot it in History, if you remember. It shoots blanks."

"Not gas pellets?" asked Ruky with an expert's eye.

Isy shrugged her shoulders. When Hagen had fired it in the classroom, it certainly wasn't gas pellets.

"My dad also used to have a pistol," threw in Amanda. "When we used to live in the West."

"You from the West?" asked Ruky, interested. "What's your old man? A Treuhand Mafioso?"

"Tax consultant."

Ruky nodded **reverently**. "Tax wheeler-dealer. Not bad. Makes his money in the East. I bet he drives a Mercedes."

"No, he doesn't," said Amanda. "Nor a Seat, either."

All three burst into laughter.

Then Ruky stubbed out his cigarette. "Changing the subject: when do I get the woolly hat?"

---

shooter – Schießeisen; dummy – Attrappe; reverently – andächtig

For a second everything was still in the kitchen. The regular ticking of the clock on the wall above the fridge seemed to be the only sound in the entire house.

Isy looked at Amanda, and Amanda looked at Isy. Should they mention that they'd frozen the evidence under a pile of slithery spaghetti? Just then the doorbell rang. It was a welcome sound to Isy. Amanda also breathed a sigh of relief. Only Ruky didn't seem too happy at the **disturbance**. Did he think the police would already be standing in front of his garden gate? He got up from his chair **edgily** and went into the veranda, where he peered through Mrs King's sparkling white lace curtains.

"Friends!" he told them with a certain sense of relief. Then they heard the veranda door open and close. They were alone.

"He's a real **fruitcake**!" said Amanda, scooping some scrambled egg into her mouth with three fingers. "You don't even find people like him in Hollywood!"

Meanwhile Isy looked around the kitchen. She spotted an unopened telegram on the sideboard, probably the message from her parents. Next to it were two oranges, a packet of cigarettes and a few cassettes of classical music. Did the Seat Nicker really listen to Mozart? He seemed to be full of **contradictions**.

---

disturbance – Störung; edgily – angespannt;
fruitcake – Früchtchen; contradiction – Widerspruch

Curious, she went into the veranda to take a look at Ruky's friends from behind the curtains. Ruky was standing at the **fence**, talking to a boy and a girl with a long, blond **pigtail**. It looked like they were arguing about something. For some reason Isy knew straightaway that the girl was Ruky's girlfriend. Her instinct had never let her down with Benedikt, either.

Just then Ruky turned away from the others to come back into the house and Isy hurried into the kitchen. She saw the damage straightaway. The only thing left of Ruky's lunch was an empty plate. Amanda's lips were gleaming with fat. "I can't take you anywhere!" said Isy appalled. "Watch out! He's coming!"

A moment later Ruky was standing in the doorway. It was obvious he wasn't going to sit back down with them.

"I have to go!" He drummed his thin fingers against the doorframe. The conversation with his two friends seemed to have made him nervous. "So, when do I get the woolly hat?"

"When are you going to tidy our room up?" countered Isy.

For a second it looked like Ruky didn't understand the question. Then he looked **coquettishly** at the tip of his sneakers. "I'll leave that to superwomen like you. Let's **settle** this **amicably**: I'm

---

fence – Zaun; pigtail – Zopf; coquettishly – kokett;
to settle sth amicably – etw. freundschaftlich regeln

throwing a party tomorrow evening! And you two are invited."

"Really?" Amanda looked like she was about to throw herself around the guy's neck. "That's **ace**! At last something's going on in this **dump**!"

Then she turned to Isy reproachfully. "You should say something, too!"

What was she supposed to say? That Ruky was extremely smart? That Amanda had **fallen for** his trick **hook, line and sinker**? Or that the woolly hat must really be valuable to him?

Instead Isy asked: "Have you got any hash at the party? I heard rumours..."

Ruky raised his hands dramatically. "You two should change your baker!" He flashed his teeth and laughed. "That **troublemaker** is going to talk me into prison. And just because I have a perfect **tan** without even having to use self-tanning lotion or the **sunbed**!"

Ruky took the packet of cigarettes from the sideboard and stuffed them into his jeans. "My father's Cuban. Nothing special about that. They used to think it was really cool here in the village. But now that they're all frustrated and **unemployed**, and people are coming back from the West to claim their properties, or both at the same time, they're flipping out. All of a sudden I'm the Turk,

---

ace – spitze; dump – Kaff; to fall for sth hook, line and sinker – voll auf etwas hereinfallen; troublemaker – Unruhestifter; tan – Bräune; sunbed – Solarium; unemployed – arbeitslos

the darkie, the black sheep. It really gets on my nerves!"

For a moment it looked like Ruky was actually about to spit in disgust onto the shiny, clean floor.

"So you didn't grow hashish?" asked Amanda, disappointed.

"If you think perfectly normal tobacco plants are hash, then yes, I grew hashish!" scoffed Ruky. "Otherwise it was just an experiment which even our biology teacher **was in on**. The leaves of tobacco plants can show raised ozone levels. They're very sensitive to ozone, and the leaves grow **discoloured**. That's the whole secret."

Ruky looked at his watch impatiently and the girls finally put on their coats. Isy had to admit that she was impressed. After meeting Ruky the Seat Nicker, Ruky had now presented himself as Ruky the **victimized** black sheep of the village and Ruky the intrepid **environmental researcher**. She couldn't help thinking of those little Russian dolls which slotted into each other. She wondered how many Rukys slotted into each other.

"And how big is the ozone hole over Green Meadows?" asked Isy derisively.

Ruky looked at her seriously. "Bloody awful as usual, if you know what I mean."

Sure she knew what he meant.

---

to be in on – Bescheid wissen; discoloured – verfärbt; to victimise – ungerecht behandeln; environmental researcher – Umweltforscher

They left the house, which Ruky carefully locked, and went their separate ways in front of the garden gate.

"See you tomorrow then! Around five!" said Ruky before he headed off towards the bus. Then he frowned and said: "Don't forget the woolly hat, girls!"

On the short walk home Amanda was in the best of moods, and she walked arm in arm with Isy. This was obviously thanks to the **forthcoming** party.

She suggested they take the woolly hat out of the refrigerator as soon as they got back, let it **thaw** and wash it so that it would be dry by the next day. She seemed set on fulfilling Ruky's wish. She'd obviously forgotten the fact that this guy had been **rummaging** through their things like a wild pig just a few hours ago.

"Isn't it great that he's giving a party?" she **went into raptures**.

"He just wants the woolly hat," said Isy. "Nothing else."

Amanda giggled. "He can have it at the drop of a hat!"

"But not from me! I'm not giving it to him!" Isy said vigorously.

Amanda froze in her steps and slipped her arm out of Isy's. "What is it now? Why do you have to

---

forthcoming – bevorstehend; to thaw – auftauen; to rummage – durchwühlen; to go into raptures – in Verzückung geraten

spoil everything? Why does everything have to go according to your head?" She looked like she was about to burst into tears of disappointment. "Give me one good reason."

The wind had brought clouds. All of a sudden they were hanging low over the village in thick, dark blankets. A short time ago, as they'd rushed over to the Kings' house, there'd been no sign of rain. Strange how quickly things could change. A big drop of rain splashed onto Isy's forehead.

"Can't you see what's going on, Amanda? They're trying to **bribe** someone. We're talking about **blackmail** here. **As hard as nails**. And if we give him the woolly hat now, we get ourselves involved, whether we like it or not." Isy's breathing was heavy and **agitated**. "I mean, we might be the calamity queens, but we're not criminals!"

---

to spoil – versauen; to bribe – erpressen; blackmail – Erpressung; as hard as nails – knallhart; agitated – aufgeregt

— 13 —

The next morning Isy was the first to wake up. She lay there **motionless** under the warm covers, listening to the rain falling softly and evenly from the lead grey sky.

It was the first night that they'd both slept through. No sweet-toothed hedgehog, no "Mr Mysterious" waking them from their sleep. Everything was as it should be. She turned pleasurably to look out of the window and thought that rain was always different wherever you went. At home she sometimes only noticed it when it was beating down against the **window-panes**. In Grandma Dora's weekend home it drummed snugly against the old **roofing felt**. Once in Bulgaria, when her dad had been given a big end-of-year bonus by the state company he used to work for and had taken them on a trip to the Black Sea, a cloud burst above them that was out of this world. Within seconds the pavements and roads were completely flooded. She'd learned the true meaning of the phrase '**bucketing down**'

---

motionless – bewegungslos; window-pane – Fensterscheibe; roofing felt – Dachpappe; to bucket down – aus Eimern schütten

in Bulgaria. The heavy downpours during the Berlin summer were nothing compared to those in the south. Isy wondered what her family were doing right now at home. Had they already had breakfast? Was Dad **coping** with the housework? And had Mum already got used to her crutches? Benedikt would, of course, already be on the way to his new girlfriend. He was making a big secret of her. The only thing they knew about her was that she was called Mascha and had **hayfever**. They'd met in the springtime at an allergy test. The pollen epidemic had bonded them.

Just as Isy had decided to make a longish call home at some point during the day, a bare foot appeared in front of her face, followed by the rest of Amanda.

Amanda sleepily shuffled to the girls' toilet in her pink slippers. When she came back she asked if they were going to go to the party styled or **casual**.

"Fifty-fifty!" decided Isy after thinking about it briefly. Then she tossed the covers to one side and got up.

After breakfast they scrubbed the rest of the floor throughout the house and started making the beds.

Amanda moaned for a while, saying she wasn't Jesus and didn't see why each pupil couldn't put his own pillow in the **pillowcase**. But after Isy had

---

to cope – zurechtkommen; hayfever – Heuschnupfen;
casual – locker, lässig; pillowcase – Kopfkissenbezug

painted the black picture of chaos that would break out if they didn't do so, Amanda gave in and followed her into the laundry and bedrooms.

Later on they ate a hot dog and Amanda started writing postcards, even though not all the beds were ready.

"Rome wasn't built in a day," she informed her friend and underlined this well-known **saying** with her customary smattering of French: "Ça suffit!"

Then she suggested surprising Trischi with a hello from Green Meadows.

She showed Isy a postcard of a **bellowing stag** in a tranquil forest **clearing** – an ideal parallel for a teacher in front of his class – and they sat down to write him holiday greetings, giggling away.

Then there was no holding Amanda back.

She **pounced on** the contents of her suitcase and spread out her clothes around the room. It soon looked like Ruky had paid another visit.

"**Take your pick!**" she said to Isy. They often exchanged clothes, though Isy usually had an advantage with her slim figure. Isy herself hadn't brought much with her, and what she had was mainly sporty. So she was happy to choose one of Amanda's white, pastel-blue embroidered blouses. It would go well with her jeans and she'd be able to tie it in a **knot** around her waist because it was too big for her.

---

saying – Sprichwort; bellowing stag – röhrender Hirsch; clearing – Lichtung; to pounce on sth – sich auf etw. stürzen; Take your pick! – Du hast die Wahl!; knot – Knoten

For a while Amanda couldn't decide between her favourite colours: violet, apple-green and pink. Then with a sigh she settled for the bright pink leggings and a baggy black T-shirt sprinkled with glitter on the neckline. The shirt was a luxury item from Italy and had ended up being too big for her mum after she'd done a crash diet. Amanda had **pinched** it straightaway. Unfortunately her mum managed to put on seven pounds over the next month and took the shirt back. It now depended on who was quicker and who knew their way around the other's hiding places better. The winner got to wear the shirt. This time, in the **muddle** of her father's broken arm and the cancelled holiday, Amanda had no problem **whipping out** the shirt from her mum's bag which she'd packed for Gran Canaria.

After choosing their clothes they went into the washroom to **raid** Amanda's toilet bag which was bulging with cosmetic samples. Although they hated lipstick and rouge, they liked making up their eyes. But as Isy's parents were particularly against that as well, Isy hardly ever used eye make-up at home.

She now **relished** coating her long eyelashes with laguna-blue mascara, and she chose a light blue, metallic eye shadow. At the neighbouring sink Amanda tried out trendy, pink eye shadow.

For some strange reason neither of them had

---

to pinch – klauen; muddle – Kuddelmuddel; to whip out – herausziehen; to raid – plündern; to relish sth – etwas genießen

even mentioned Ruky's name that day. Since their conversation about the woolly hat yesterday, they had been completely **incommunicado**.

Isy watched Amanda spray a lilac streak in the fringe of her blond **crew cut**.

Maybe her argument about not wanting to become a criminal herself had convinced Amanda. It was equally possible that Amanda would pull it off to go to the party in a huff with the frozen spaghetti under her arm.

In any case they were now so made-up that even Trischi would have addressed them as "Miss" on the street.

As they took their coats off the **pegs** in the hall, Amanda took the initiative to talk about the woolly hat.

"So what are we going to do then?" she asked, without even mentioning the words 'woolly hat'. "Shall we take it with us?"

As she saw Isy's **dismissive expression** she added bitterly: "I think it's pretty stupid that you always think you're responsible for other people. Really! You could be wrong. Maybe he doesn't want to blackmail anybody. Maybe there's just a reward out for it."

That was a good point. Isy hadn't thought of that! Without saying a word she went into the kitchen and took the frozen bowl out of the refri-

---

incommunicado – isoliert; crew cut – Stoppelfrisur; peg – Haken; dismissive expression – abweisende Miene

gerator. The shiny metal immediately **misted up**. It would be a while before Ruky could fish his evidence out of the noodles and clean it up. But that wouldn't be too much **hassle** for him with the **prospect** of a sizeable reward!

---

to mist up – beschlagen; hassle – Mühe; prospect – Aussicht

— 14 —

Amanda seemed to **float** on the short walk to Ruky's house. "He'll think we've made a noodle salad for the party!" she speculated and relished the surprise in advance.

The rain had **eased off** a bit. It was now mostly dripping from the trees. Isy thought of the old saying: it always rains twice under trees. Sometimes that was true.

By the time they knocked on Ruky's brown veranda door, their hearts were thumping a little, too. What was this party going to be like? Would there be other interesting guys like Ruky?

Isy knew a blond girl with pigtail would be there for sure. She hadn't forgotten her.

"Hey, knock again!" urged Amanda when no one answered. "He must **be hard of hearing**!"

But no matter how much they tried, they couldn't get anyone to open the door. All was quiet in the house. Strange. Why wasn't Ruky there? Had they got the time wrong? Were they too early?

---

to float – schweben; to ease off – nachlassen;
to be hard of hearing – schwerhörig sein

Isy briskly pushed down the door handle. The door was locked. "No go!" she said to Amanda, going up the few steps to the veranda. Amanda looked like a deflated balloon. Her hope of a good party had been blown away.

"Things like this don't even happen in Hollywood!" she mumbled **distraughtly**. "You don't actually think he forgot the party?"

"I doubt it. But can you see anyone else here apart from us?"

Strange party if no one was there! Something had gone seriously wrong. What's more, it was cold and unpleasant standing outside. Isy rummaged around in her coat pocket and pulled out the **bunch of keys** from the school lodge. There were a number of other keys on the ring.

"Do you think one of them **fits** here?" Amanda asked hopefully, hopping from one leg to the next, fighting the cold. Within a fraction of a second she seemed **mortified** by the thought. "We can't just go inside!"

"What did he do at our place?" asked Isy disrespectfully. "Or are you planning **to grow roots** until nightfall?"

She tried out a number of keys on the key ring. The sixth or seventh fitted the lock. She opened the veranda door effortlessly. His mum's private keys were also on the key ring Ruky had given them.

---

distraughtly – verstört; bunch of keys – Schlüsselbund; to fit – passen; mortified – beschämt; to grow roots – Wurzeln schlagen

Isy couldn't shake off a certain **apprehension** as she entered the unfamiliar house with Amanda. All was quiet, and the smell of fried potatoes and stale cigarette smoke still hung in the air. They walked timidly through to the kitchen. No, it didn't look like someone had thrown a party here!

Their noses had been right: the frying pan with the remains of the fried potatoes was still on the stove. An open packet of cigarettes was on the table and the dishes in the sink had been washed up thoroughly. Ruky seemed to be a very tidy person. Isy didn't like to think what the kitchen at home would look like if she was alone in the flat for a few days.

Her parents' telegram was still lying unopened on the sideboard. Only the oranges had disappeared.

Amanda tossed her coat over the back of a chair, slipped the last two fried potatoes into her mouth, and went over to the window where she poked her finger into the pot of a medium-sized **myrtle**. "Could do with some water!" she ascertained. Then they sat down at the kitchen table, just like the day before, and listened to two **blackbirds** fighting over the best bed for the night. Evenings in the countryside had completely different sounds to those in the city. In Berlin they'd be hearing the monotonous roar of **homeward-bound** cars and buses right up into their flat. Every now and again there'd be the

---

apprehension – Besorgnis/Beklemmung; myrtle – Myrthe; blackbird – Amsel; homeward bound – heimwärts strebend

sound of screeching brakes or a shrill siren. Admittedly, Berlin wasn't New York, that bubbling **cauldron** that they'd seen on TV, but it wasn't the quietest city on the planet, either.

After darkness had fallen over the garden, the girls turned on the lights and wandered through the house. They didn't dare go into the rooms on the top floor, but they were curious to take a closer look at the sitting room downstairs. It wasn't very big, but the way it was neatly **furnished** made it look bigger. Isy liked the two small sofas most of all. They both had a colourful, flowery pattern and stood opposite each other. When the girls went back into the kitchen, Amanda hungrily tore open the fridge door. All she found was a solitary yoghurt, three eggs, half a lump of butter and a packet of sliced bread.

"**I'll eat my hat if** he was going to give a party!"

Furious, she slammed the fridge door.

"Let's go, Amanda!" said Isy. Well, it was true: no Ruky, no partygoers, not even a little hot dog or a bite of potato salad. Not even a measly coke. They were, to use an old joke, not just super, they were **superfluous**. Amanda, however, flopped into one of the kitchen chairs.

"I'm staying!" she announced doggedly. "Even if I have to die of hunger!"

Just then the bell rang. The girls sat up as if

---

cauldron – Kessel; furnished – eingerichtet; I'll eat my hat – Ich fresse einen Besen; superfluous – überflüssig

they'd been given an **electric shock**. But why should Ruky ring at his own house? It was probably the first party guests. They rushed over to the veranda. A young man was walking up the poorly lit garden path wearing a green overall. He had a **badge** with the words "Party Service" on his breast pocket.

"The King household?" he asked in a friendly manner. "Party Service Hermann! Sorry for the **delay**, but our **delivery van** had a breakdown this afternoon. I've brought a small selection of cold dishes with me, as much as I could get into my private car, but there should be something for everyone!"

"The Kings aren't here. Could you come again another time?" asked Isy politely.

"That could be difficult," said the man from the party service hesitantly. He was around thirty and he wore his blond hair in a short ponytail. It looked like the tail of a duck. Isy had a nickname for him straightaway: The **Drake**!

"All the afternoon deliveries have been delayed because of the breakdown. I won't be able to make it back for two or three hours. I expect that's too late for the Kings…"

"What did the Kings order?" Amanda chipped into the conversation.

"The young man didn't want to choose any-

---

electric shock – Stromschlag; badge – Abzeichen;
delay – Verspätung; delivery van – Lieferwagen; drake – Erpel

thing on the phone. And as he didn't have our catalogue, we agreed he'd make a selection when I came around." The Drake smiled charmingly. "We have a really great choice. Loads of delicious dishes! Maybe you'd like to take a look yourself?" He made a move towards the garden gate where he'd presumably parked the car full of tasty snacks.

"I'm coming!" called Amanda, pushing past Isy hastily. "You've saved us! We were just about **to starve**!"

"But we haven't got any money with us!" called Isy after her. Then she went back into the house. Hopefully Amanda wouldn't **get up to** any **mischief**. Who knows if Ruky wanted her choosing the dishes? Isy had an uneasy feeling. What an extravagance! She didn't know anyone who booked expensive party services for teenage parties. Was Ruky a **show-off**? Or was the woolly hat worth so much that he could throw his cash around like this?

She would have preferred to have **fetched** Amanda **back**, but it was too late for that. Her friend came back into the kitchen triumphantly balancing an aluminium **tray** full of delicious snacks. She put it onto the table with bated breath. Isy stared gobsmacked at the spread: roasted meat, tongue, ham, chicken, salami, cheese and tasty salads lavishly garnished with blue grapes, slices of pineapple and

---

to starve – verhungern; to get up to mischief – Dummheiten machen; show-off – Angeber; to fetch back – zurückholen; tray – Tablett

halved cherries. It was all far too nicely done just to wolf down! "The number one dish on offer!" announced Amanda proudly, slipping a blue grape into her mouth. "It's called 'Fireplace Feast'. But I think we can manage it without a fireplace!"

Isy couldn't help laughing, though she tried not to. "And how much did it cost?"

"Nothing. The bill's in the post."

"Ruky will be pleased to get that!"

"Why not? He ordered the service **in the first place**!"

"But not the most expensive dish!"

"Oh, come on! It wasn't much more expensive than the others," said Amanda as she started to look for knives and forks. "At least we now know that he *was* planning to give a party and was **expecting** us."

She found some white plates with a pastel blue **rim** in the lower section of the kitchen sideboard and put them on the table. "Do you think there'll be more than five guests?"

Isy shrugged her shoulders. "Doesn't look like it at the moment. Most of them are probably still on holiday."

After they'd taken a look for drinks and not found any, they sat back down at the table to wait. They pricked up their ears at every sound and every rustle, and jumped to their feet whenever they heard someone walking past on the street. But no

---

in the first place – überhaupt erst, extra; to expect – erwarten; rim – Rand

one came. It was the **weirdest** party they'd ever been to!

As the big hand on the kitchen clock crept up to half past seven, Amanda reached out **decisively** for a chicken leg. She was expecting Isy to stop her with a loud protest, but Isy said nothing. Even as Amanda started piling salad, juicy roast beef, slices of cheese and fruit onto her plate, Isy didn't interfere. She was suspicious about the whole situation. Why didn't Ruky come? Where were his friends? Where was the boy who Ruky had spoken with the day before over the garden fence? Or the girl with the blond pigtail?

She looked at the **wasteful** extravagance of the cold platter which was **taking** some serious **punishment** at the hands of Amanda's **onslaught**. Ruky's generosity **baffled** her. What if this wasn't meant for Amanda and her?

In the end Amanda took the initiative and piled cheese and roasted meat onto Isy's plate.

"Eat something! We'll never get a chance like this again!"

At first Isy ate hesitantly, but after a while she started enjoying the food to her heart's content. Maybe Amanda was right. Strange how she hadn't even noticed how hungry she was.

When their stomachs were full and Amanda

---

weird – komisch/merkwürdig; decisively – entschlossen; wasteful – verschwenderisch; to take punishment – leiden unter; onslaught – Ansturm; to baffle – verwirren

announced with a pleasant grunt that she was about to **burst** with a loud bang, they put a plate on top of the remains and put the platter into the fridge. The generous **benefactor** should at least have a decent breakfast!

Then they looked through the kitchen drawers for a pen and paper, and wrote a note for Ruky. They thanked him for the delicious dinner, explained how they had got into his house, and didn't hide their disappointment that he hadn't turned up all evening. After they'd promised they'd call around the next day, they **signed off**. They washed up their dishes, put everything back in its place and swept the last crumbs from the table. Before they put their coats on, Amanda gave the myrtle a drop of water.

It was around 9 o'clock in the evening when they took the bowl of frozen spaghetti with the woolly hat out of the fridge, turned off the lights and carefully locked the door. Goodness knows when their **host** was going to come home!

In the lodge's white tiled washroom they jumped under the shower giggling. They washed away all their pretty colours and all their expectations about the party. As they did so, they talked about where Ruky could have got to.

"He nicked a Seat and is on the run!" gurgled Amanda as she washed the **dye** out of her hair.

---

to burst – platzen; benefactor – Spender/Wohltäter; to sign off – sich verabschieden; host – Gastgeber; dye – Färbemittel

"He's spent the night on a **raised hide** somewhere and is starving hungry!" spluttered Isy. In the simmering haze of the showers they laughed themselves silly, but Isy couldn't get rid of the feeling that Ruky **was in hot water**. He'd **got himself landed in** something. He'd been so keen about getting his hands on the woolly hat, he wouldn't have just **blown the chance** to get it from them today! By tomorrow they'd be a bit the **wiser**.

---

raised hide – Hochsitz; to be in hot water – in der Tinte sitzen;
to get oneself landed in sth – sich etwas einbrocken;
to blow the chance – sich eine Gelegenheit entgehen lassen;
wiser – klüger

— 15 —

The next day, straight after a quick breakfast, they called Ruky. They let the phone ring for a long time, but no one answered.

"Maybe he's still asleep," suggested Amanda, who also liked to **have a lie-in**.

"Maybe he's on the move again," said Isy, who liked to be out and about early.

They tried to call him again half an hour later, and when he still didn't answer, they decided to go over and take a look.

This time they didn't even bother knocking at the veranda door. They just unlocked it straightaway.

They stopped in the doorway out of **politeness**, calling out Ruky's name and hoping for a reply. But there wasn't a sound throughout the whole house, just like the day before.

Isy led the way into the kitchen. Nothing had changed since their last visit. Their note for Ruky was still on the kitchen table.

They didn't even bother to look in the fridge to

---

to have a lie-in – ausschlafen; politeness – Höflichkeit

see if the 'fireplace feast' had been left **untouched**. Ruky hadn't come home.

"What now?" asked Amanda, flopping down heftily onto a blue plastic stool which Mrs King used for her kitchen duties. "Do you **get** what's going on?"

What was there to 'get'? For some reason or another Ruky hadn't come home. There could be various explanations. The police might be one of them, but there was no sign of the police for miles around. If, on the other hand, he had tracked down the owner of the grey Seat and was planning to blackmail him, then…

"Maybe someone kidnapped him," said Amanda, interrupting Isy's thoughts. For a person who preferred love stories to thrillers, that was a pretty sharp idea.

"Okay! Let's search the house!"

Amanda opened her eyes wide. "The house? But why?"

"Maybe we'll find something. A name, a telephone number, some clue. How can we help him if we don't even know where to begin?" asked Isy earnestly. Amanda could understand that.

They started on the top floor. The blue tiled bathroom was small and, apart from the standard mirrored cabinet and a laundry basket, there was no other place to hide a **message**.

---

untouched – unberührt; to get – verstehen;
message – Nachricht

Isy started checking through the medicine cabinet and told Amanda to check Mrs King's cosmetics. Fortunately for Amanda, Mrs King didn't seem to be as much as a cosmetic freak as her mum. Instead of endless tubes and jars she only found a night cream, a half-used bottle of cologne and the remains of a tinted day cream. Then she checked the laundry basket, which didn't give anything away except for a few gym shirts, two T-shirts and a lot of coloured socks belonging to Ruky.

Although Isy found it rather unpleasant **invading** the Kings' private sphere, she inspected the numerous **ointments** and boxes of tablets which she knew from the thrillers she'd seen on TV. It was here that the hero nearly always found the microfilm in the empty tube of toothpaste after a long, **thorough** search. But what had to be, had to be.

After the last packet of green stomach drops also failed to shed any light on Ruky's secret, they set about the two rooms in the attic. The first, presumably Mrs King's bedroom, was locked. The second, however, was a tiny room and was clearly Ruky's **realm**. The first thing they both noticed here was its tidiness. Back home, if Isy wanted to go into Benedikt's room, she had to clear a path first with her feet.

Apart from an old **daybed** with piled up bedding, a light wardrobe and a bookcase, there was

---

to invade – eindringen; ointment – Salbe; thorough – gründlich; realm – [König]reich; daybed – Liege

only a work top on **trestles** with an up-to-date PC in the room. While Amanda checked it out, Isy looked through the books. This was one of the most popular places for messages. Ruky's literary wealth consisted almost completely of **non-fiction books** on the topics of biology and IT. But he also had some adventure books, like the ones Benedikt had.

He even had a few fairy tale stories from his early years. Isy was pleased to see some familiar names. That was something she and Amanda had **realised** with astonishment when they first became friends: they hadn't just grown up in different political systems, they'd also grown up in a different world of books.

Isy didn't know the Robber Hotzenplotz and the Children of Bullerbü, and Amanda had never heard of the Wizard of Oz or Alfons Zitterbacke. They swapped 'Alice in Wonderland' for 'The Island of Swans', 'Pippi Longstocking' for 'Timur and his Gang'. For a while 'Never Ending Story' was Isy's favourite book, and Amanda read 'Four-legged Friends' three times and asked for a **lioness** like Kinuli for her birthday. Nowadays they were both into slightly less childish books: Amanda preferred to bury herself in romance novels and Isy consumed thrillers **by the crate**. But when a children's book was particularly exciting or funny they'd go back to their old ways.

---

trestle – [Auflage]bock; non-fiction books – Sachbücher;
to realise – feststellen; lioness – Löwin; by the crate – kistenweise

Isy carefully **flicked through** each of Ruky's books from the front to the back cover, or shook them slightly in the hope of finding a note, a letter, or something that would give them a clue about Ruky's **disappearance**. She reckoned he was too smart not to have **covered himself** in some way. But the bookcase proved to be a waste of time. Disappointed, she put the books back onto the shelves.

"I wouldn't say no if you wanted to **lend** me **a hand**!" she said to Amanda who had turned on the computer and was toying at the keyboard.

"I am," she said smartly. "Give me a word with five letters!"

"Why?"

"Because I want to try and crack a password. We might get a message if it works."

Flabbergasted Isy left her **comfy** cross-legged position on the floor and peered over Amanda's shoulder. "Are you trying to tell me that Ruky might have been keeping information in his computer?"

"Sure. He could hardly keep his secret safer than with a good password."

"Amanda!" cried Isy. "I could kiss you!" And then she added with a giggle: "Even if I'm not Prince Charles."

"Typical Isy!" mumbled Amanda, infuriated. "Think, girl! A word with five letters!"

---

to flick through – durchblättern; disappearance – Verschwinden; to cover oneself – sich absichern; to lend a hand – helfen; flabbergasted – verblüfft; comfy – bequem

"Theft!" cried Isy like a shot. "Theft's got exactly five letters. Go on, I bet it works!"

Amanda's fingers darted over the keyboard, but "theft" didn't crack the code.

"Doesn't work. Another word, please!"

"Crime!" That had to be it. It had five letters and hit the nail right on the head. Ruky **was bound** to have chosen it for his password.

"Doesn't work either!" said Amanda after a quick look at the screen. "No response. Keep going!"

Keep going? For how long? How many words there were with five letters? Isy stared despairingly at Ruky's flickering monitor. If she only knew what hobbies he had, what his favourite colours were, his favourite animal or favourite song! There were thousands of **possibilities** to choose a password from your own life. For Ruky, for Amanda, for her.

"There's no point", said Isy, disappointed. "We don't know enough about him. His password is bound to have a personal connection. We might as well look for a **needle in a haystack**!"

They decided to head back to the lodge for the time being and write down anything they could think of that had five letters and something to do with Ruky.

"Do you really think he's in danger?" asked Amanda as they went down the creaking stairs.

---

theft – Diebstahl; to be bound to – etw. bestimmt tun; possibility – Möglichkeit; needle in a haystack – Nadel im Heuhaufen

"Only if he really did use the woolly hat to try and blackmail the owner of the Seat. But as long as the guy doesn't have the woolly hat he won't do anything to Ruky. He'll probably come here to look for it."

"Here?" asked Amanda horrified. "Why didn't you say that before?"

"You didn't ask me before!"

Amanda looked like she was going to rush out of the house on the spot. "I'm going to flip out if he comes here!"

Isy had to laugh. "Do you think he's going to break and enter in the middle of the day? Anyway, maybe we've got the wrong end of the stick, and Ruky just broke his leg on the way to his grandma's, or ran off with his girlfriend, and we're **getting worked up** about him for nothing."

"Worked up is an understatement," said Amanda, disappearing into the kitchen with a sigh. Isy's last words sounded quite **reassuring**, thank goodness. Why always think the worst? She'd already calmed down a bit as she opened the fridge door. It bothered her to think that the tasty snacks they'd left for Ruky's breakfast were going to waste.

"What do you **reckon**?" she called Isy, who had disappeared into the tiny guest's toilet. "Should we take the **leftovers** with us?"

Without waiting for Isy's reply, Amanda took

---

to get worked up – sich einen Kopf machen; reassuring – beruhigend; to reckon – meinen; leftovers – Reste

the 'fireplace feast' out of the fridge and started looking for some **grease-proof paper**. Amanda knew such things were usually kept in a trusty kitchen drawer together with aluminium foil, cling film, tin-openers and a small plastic bag where the housewife kept the grey, black and auburn rubber seals from jars of fine herbs.

She froze as she opened the fourth drawer next to the sink. She thought she'd heard footsteps in front of the house. Paralyzed with fear, she rushed into the corridor and bumped into Isy, who had also heard the noise.

Both were as silent and pale as **wax figures**. They stood there, in some stranger's house, listening apprehensively to the footsteps going up the front steps, and the sound of a key being turned cautiously in the lock of the veranda door. Whoever it might be, it certainly wasn't Ruky King! Even Ruky's mother, if she'd come back from her trip, wouldn't **creep** into her own house as mysteriously as that.

Isy instinctively dragged Amanda into the sitting room, pushed her under the right-hand sofa, and disappeared under the left one. They lay there, squashed up against the floor, as quiet as mice, their hearts pounding, **sweating** with fear, terrified that the intruder might hear it trickling down their backs.

---

grease-proof paper – Pergamentpapier; wax figure – Wachsfigur; to creep – kriechen; to sweat – schwitzen

For a while the only thing they could hear were his footsteps. Footsteps moving cautiously up to the top floor and disappearing without faltering into the room where they themselves had been only a few minutes before.

They heard the stranger's footsteps creaking above them as he paced up and down. He was searching Ruky's room for the woolly hat. **A clear-cut case**. They'd guessed right.

As if through a **veil** of fear Isy saw Amanda trying to clamber out from underneath the sofa, looking like a helpless **turtle**.

"Are you out of your mind?" she hissed. "Stay where you are!"

"I can't breathe!" whimpered Amanda. "I have to get out of here! Let's make a run for it while he's still upstairs!"

Just then Ruky's bedroom door closed and the footsteps started coming down the stairs.

Trembling, Amanda dived back under her protective **shell**. She just managed to get her left leg under the sofa before the sitting room door opened and the stranger walked past the sofa to the wall unit at the end of the room.

Isy saw his dark blue jeans and large sneakers. The edges of the shoes looked strange, like they'd been chewed. After that, all she could do was listen to what happened.

---

a clear-cut case – ein eindeutiger Fall; veil – Schleier; turtle – Schildkröte; shell – Gehäuse

The unit doors and drawers were opened and shut. The stranger briefly **cleared** his **throat**. He sounded like a smoker. Then there was a moment's silence before the huge sneakers, this time on Amanda's side, walked past the sofa.

All she could see from her perspective now were the stranger's legs as he disappeared into the corridor and out of the house. The girls could clearly hear him locking the door and walking down the garden path.

"Amanda?" whispered Isy. "Amanda?"

There was a sign of life underneath the opposite sofa.

"Oooohhhh!" groaned Amanda. "I thought I was going to **faint**! He almost stood on my nose!"

"He wouldn't have done it on purpose. Not if I know him."

A **dull thud** indicated that Amanda had banged her head. She rubbed her forehead in pain.

"Are you trying to say you know him?" she asked in disbelief.

"I recognised his shoes."

"But everybody wears sneakers like that!"

"Not like these ones. They have a very **distinguishing feature**," said Isy sadly. "You don't have to believe me."

"Don't worry. I won't!"

---

to clear one's throat – sich räuspern; to faint – ohnmächtig werden; dull thud – dumpfer Schlag; distinguishing feature – besonderes Kennzeichen

Amanda looked like she thought Isy was mad. She brushed down her leggings and threw herself onto the sofa, exhausted. Then her curiosity **got the better of** her.

"Okay, who, in your opinion, do you think it was then?"

"It was," said Isy with a big sigh of disappointment. "Someone I'd never have expected: Mr Rimpau!"

---

to get the better of – die Oberhand gewinnen/siegen

— 16 —

Sometimes, when Isy went walking with her parents in the woods, her dad would spontaneously put his arms around a tree. It might be a beech tree with smooth, silvery skin, or a pine tree with its rough **bark**: whatever. The main thing was, the tree felt his friendship.

At the beginning the family had laughed at him, but bit by bit they'd also started **timidly** giving a **chestnut tree** a friendly slap as they passed, or putting their arm around a birch. It was a funny, mysterious feeling, hugging a tree. Did it really feel anything? Did it actually sense the warmth of the body or the beating heart?

After the mad episode with Mr Rimpau's secret visit to the Kings' house, Isy had tried to **persuade** her friend to **take a stroll** with her through the woods for once. Just to walk and get some fresh air, and sort out the thoughts which were fluttering chaotically around her head like headless chickens. But Amanda wanted to stay in the lodge. She'd

---

bark – Rinde; timidly – zaghaft; chestnut tree – Kastanienbaum; to persuade – überreden; to take a stroll – spazieren gehen

probably sat down in front of the TV with the remaining cold platter and thought about whether Mr Rimpau himself had done all the crimes he wrote about in his books. After the **initial** shock she seemed to find this thought extremely exciting.

And so Isy set off alone along the wide sandy path through the chestnut trees, the oaks and the auburn beeches. The air smelled a bit of nuts and cinnamon, and it was quiet in the forest. A blackbird occasionally darted noisily through the **undergrowth**.

Normally Isy would have used the walk to look out for mushrooms. But now all she could think about were Mr Rimpau's blasted sneakers, Alfredo's favourite chewing toy.

What had he been up to in Ruky's house? That was the first, big question. The second question was: why hadn't he waited until it was dark to make his secret visit? He'd taken the risk of being seen by the neighbours both on entering and leaving the house. A real **crook** would never be so stupid. Neither would a **shrewd** writer of thrillers. And anyway, could a man who was as incredibly nice as Mr Rimpau really have two faces?

Of course, Isy knew from innumerable thrillers that, by the end of the story, the nicest people usually **turned out to be** the nastiest rascals. And Alfredo's master had a special touch for such people.

---

initial – anfänglich; undergrowth – Unterholz; crook – Gauner; shrewd – gewieft; to turn out to be – sich entpuppen als

Of course, they'd have to find out what the writer had to do with the whole thing. That wouldn't be an easy job. But they didn't have a choice if they wanted to help Ruky. And there was something else they'd have to find out about.

Where were Ruky's friends? Where was the girl with the blond pigtail? Isy had the feeling that the way to find Ruky was through a friend. They had to be somewhere in Green Meadows! An idea shot through Isy's head. What was the mysterious prophecy about the lodge which the older students had mentioned a few times?

Bloodthirsty bats, like tiny vampires, flattering about on mild summer evenings; owls darting into their nests in the old fireplaces; and in the attic, which was permanently locked, a woman, who appeared to be no more than white mist, got up to her foul deeds. A treasure lay hidden in the cellar, buried by three robbers. Then came the thing about the magic cap of invisibility and the gold. Of course Isy didn't believe in such **idle gossip**, but she did find that 'magic cap', even if it was just a woollen hat. The cut-up woolly hat had disguised a man who had robbed the post office. But what about the story with the three robbers? Maybe Ruky hadn't been alone in the Seat? Maybe the three of them had stolen the car and found the woolly hat in the glove compartment? Maybe Ruky was just **covering for** the other two?

---

idle gossip – leeres Geschwätz; to cover for sb – jmd. decken

Maybe the boy at the fence and the pigtailed girl were in it from the start?

What an exciting thought! But it wasn't impossible…

At an oak tree where the clear October light shone through the mighty, half-stripped branches like pure gold onto the forest floor, Isy turned around and set off home. Amanda would be getting **impatient**.

Amanda wasn't sitting in front of the TV as Isy had expected. She was lying on her bed on her stomach, reading. When Isy came into the room, she put her magazine to one side and sat up.

"Guess who called!"

"Ruky?"

Amanda shook her head.

"Not Mr Rimpau?!"

"Can't you think about anything else?" Her friend rolled her eyes. "Trischi called!"

Dr. Trischi! Here? Well, what a surprise! For a moment Isy **regretted** not having been there. "What did he want?"

"He'd just come back from Denmark because his son got mumps, and he found our postcard in his letterbox. He said he **was** completely **bowled over**! You and me in Green Meadows, the saving angels of 6b!" Amanda laughed. "Seems he didn't think we were up to it. Anyway he called our parents straight

---

impatient – ungeduldig; to regret – etwas bedauern;
to be bowled over – sprachlos sein

away to find out more. He said he'd come to Green Meadows without delay if we need help. We just have to call him!" She made a short, mysterious pause. "But I told him everything was under control here and we'd **manage** the rest on our own. I said he should come on Monday with the others."

What? Already? But that was in just four days time! Stunned, Isy quickly began **to do** her **sums**. It was true! The day after the day after tomorrow, the whole of Year Six would be **bustling around** here, occupying the house from the attic to the cellar. Then they could completely forget their rescue mission for Ruky. They'd have to **re-adjust** to community life and there'd be no freedom to undertake such activities. Unbelievable, how the time had flown by! How the devil were they meant to solve this blasted case so quickly?

"Oh, yeah," remembered Amanda. "I told Trischi that we were going to have a writer reading from his work here next week. Provided Mr Rimpau isn't already in prison." She fell silent, uncomfortable at the thought.

"Mr Rimpau in prison? Are you off your rocker?"

"But you said yourself that..."

"Okay. Sure. He was in Ruky's house, and he's almost definitely got something to do with the whole thing. But that doesn't mean he robbed the

---

to manage – schaffen; to do sums – rechnen; to bustle around – herumwuseln; to re-adjust – sich einfügen post office!" Isy glared at Amanda, **exasperated**. "Do you know what I think? I think the best thing would be if we just asked him ourselves."

Amanda slipped down off her bed. "Okay. Then let's ask him!"

"And how do you suggest we do that? Do you want to tell him that we were under the sofa when he was round at Ruky's?"

"Do we have to say that?"

No, they didn't. But they couldn't just **barge in** there either. If they did do it, then they'd have to be exceptionally clever. Above all they needed a **pre-text**, a reason to get Mr Rimpau into the lodge. And it needed to be **watertight**. They didn't want to arouse the writer's suspicions.

"So how are we meant to get him here?" asked Isy. "Do you think he'll come without a good reason?"

"First of all I have to eat something," said Amanda. "I can't think on an empty stomach!"

They went down to the kitchen and Amanda started dishing out the rest of the 'fireplace feast' onto two plates. It still all looked really tasty.

"Sausage or rice salad?" asked Amanda, waving the spoon. "Smoked pork or chicken?"

"I'll have a small piece of the 'Goldbroiler'!" Isy pointed at a piece of roast chicken. Amanda snorted with laughter.

---

exasperated – verärgert; to barge in – herausplatzen;
pretext – Vorwand; watertight – wasserdicht

"Goldbroiler! That's some word! Like, like 'Datsche' for a weekend house or 'Kaderleiter' for personnel manager! Or 'Kaufhalle' for supermarket! No, really, you had some funny words!"

"Now we have some even funnier ones! Like 'outfit' for clothes, or that stupid word 'kids' for children. Why does everybody suddenly start saying it without thinking? A real 'Kitz' is spelt with 'tz' in German and is the **offspring** of a deer!"

"But kids is English!"

"Exactly. Why do we have to talk English with each other? I think it's awful!"

"It doesn't bother me. I grew up with it", admitted Amanda.

"I grew up with it as well," insisted Isy stubbornly, but then she gave a conciliatory smile. "'Goldbroiler' really is a stupid word!"

Then they tucked into their food.

Beyond the kitchen window the first soft shadows of dusk were settling over the garden. It was getting dark earlier every day.

"I've got an idea," said Amanda with her mouth full. "What you do think if I called him and asked him to write something in my **autograph book**?"

"I don't know," said Isy, shaking her head. "He could do that when he does the reading next week. He won't come over here just for that."

"Then we'll have to think of something more dramatic."

---

offspring – Junges; autograph book – Poesiealbum

"That's what I mean. A real disaster!"

They giggled. But Isy **lingered** on the subject. Hadn't Mr Rimpau himself said something along those lines? What did he say jokingly just before saying goodbye? They should call him in the case of flooding, a power cut or a forest fire! That's exactly what he said. He'd **unintentionally** given them the **cue**. Of course there was nothing they could do about flooding or a forest fire, but a power cut would be as **easy as pie**.

"Amanda", said Isy. "I know what we can do. The countdown is on!"

---

to linger – beharren; unintentionally – unabsichtlich; cue – Stichwort; easy as pie – kinderleicht

— 17 —

At a quarter to seven they switched off the **fuses** in the cellar. At twelve minutes to seven, they dialled Mr Rimpau's telephone number in the light of a candle.

At seven on the dot they heard his Golf **pull up** abruptly in front of the lodge. They'd done it.

"Don't forget: all our questions have to sound **casual**!" Isy whispered to Amanda. "He mustn't suspect anything!" Then she took the candle off the table in order to shed some light on their guest's arrival. If she hadn't been so nervous, she would have found the situation extremely atmospheric. The way she was feeling, she was startled on seeing her own enormous shadow in the hall.

"How did you manage it?" Mr Rimpau immediately asked before disappearing with Alfredo into the cellar. "Did you overload the **mains supply**?"

"No idea," lied Isy. "We don't even know where the fuse box is!"

At four minutes past seven the lights were on

---

fuse – Sicherung; to pull up – [heranfahren und] anhalten; casual – beiläufig; mains supply – Stromnetz again. Mr Rimpau celebrated his victory over the electricity supply with a freshly filled pipe on the third chair in the kitchen. It was a mystery to him how many **safety catches** could spring all at the same time. But at the end of the day he was a storyteller, not an electrician, and he doubted the old mains supply at the lodge had been kept up to date.

At seven minutes past seven Amanda made Mr Rimpau a cup of her famous "tea à la Moscou". After all, the electricity was back on.

At eleven minutes past seven Isy started having a cosy chat with their guest while tickling Alfredo's brawny neck as he lay comfortably at her feet.

They talked about school, and Mr Rimpau expressed his **conviction** that teaching would have to change fundamentally in the coming years. In his opinion computers should play a major role in schools. Amanda agreed with him enthusiastically. It had always been her dream to be connected with the teacher via a computer from her sofa.

Isy couldn't imagine that. Everybody at home with their own screen? Who could you **gossip** with then? What would happen to interaction, **common ground**?

Only when Amanda cleared her throat did Isy remember it was time to bring Ruky's name into play.

---

safety catch – Sicherung; conviction – Überzeugung;
to gossip – tratschen; common ground – Gemeinsamkeit

At seven twenty Mr Rimpau admitted knowing Ruky King. Yes, very well, in fact.

"That **lad** has got all my classical music cassettes!" he revealed with a grin. "I hope the experiment worked out!"

At seven twenty-four Isy and Amanda found out that Ruky had spent the entire summer exposing his vegetables to a constant stream of Bach, Beethoven, Händel and other Greats. He'd heard that English and Canadian biologists had discovered that plants reacted very **sensitively** to music and grew more quickly. Since then he'd put his tape player in the vegetable patch and delighted the lettuce and **parsley** with Mozart, spoiled the beans with Vivaldi, and delighted the pumpkins with Haydn. The tomatoes had turned out to be real opera lovers with a particular **predilection** for Verdi.

Isy would probably have thought Mr Rimpau was **pulling** their **legs** if she hadn't seen the cassettes on the sideboard in the kitchen and the impressive pumpkins in Ruky's garden. And that was all because of Haydn?

Amanda also looked more than sceptical.

"And how do they respond to Rock?" she asked warily.

Mr Rimpau shrugged his shoulders. "I can only say what Ruky said. He told me plants don't like aggressive music. Heavy Metal kills them!"

---

lad – Bursche; sensitive – empfindlich; parsley – Petersilie; predilection – Vorliebe; to pull sb's leg – jmd. aufziehen

"It's the other way round for me!" said Amanda, and all three of them laughed.

At seven thirty they showed Mr Rimpau around the house. They decided to hold the reading in the spacious dining room rather than the recreation room. The girls had only used the dining room once, and they'd felt so lost in there that, from then on, they'd decided to eat in the kitchen.

At seven thirty-five Isy put the decisive question to Mr Rimpau. She casually mentioned that she'd seen him in the village High Street earlier on in the day. He'd been parking his car in front of the King's house, but he hadn't responded to her friendly wave. Hadn't he seen her?

At seven thirty-six Mr Rimpau **lied**.

He claimed he hadn't been in Green Meadows all day. He'd spent the entire day at his desk, writing an article for a newspaper.

At seven thirty-seven Isy glanced at his blue sneakers with the chewed-up edges and asked, "Do you ever **lend** them to anyone?"

The writer shook his head in surprise. "Like who? They don't fit anyone **apart from** me. Not everybody has got such big feet!" Then he thanked Amanda for the tea and whistled to Alfredo. He had guests in his weekend house and, as his wife was at their flat in town, he didn't want to leave them waiting any longer.

At seven thirty-eight Amanda thought of her

---

to lie – lügen; to lend – etwas ausleihen; apart from – außer

autograph book. She rushed upstairs to get it so that Mr Rimpau could write something in it. In the meantime Isy thanked him for his help. Fortunately she thought of something which might save Mr Rimpau's **honour**.

"Do you know anyone in Green Meadows or the local area who drives a grey Seat?"

"Yes," said the writer straight away. "My wife!"

At seven forty-one Mr Rimpau patiently wrote a few lyrical lines in Amanda's pink autograph book while standing in the doorway. At seven forty-four he sped off in his Golf.

At seven forty-five and a half, Isy and Amanda read his **entry** with bright red faces. He'd seen right through them. A saying by Wilhelm Busch was emblazoned in Amanda's book:

He who looks with eyes of suspicion,
*sees his worst nightmare **come to fruition**!*

---

honour – Ehre; entry – Eintrag;
to come to fruition – sich verwirklichen

— 18 —

You could look at it whichever way you wanted: Mr Rimpau was still under suspicion. A **prime suspect** even.

"He's **lying through his teeth**!" marvelled Amanda while making herself another ham sandwich. "So much for spending all day at his desk! I suppose it was a ghost wearing his sneakers then!"

Isy **was down in the dumps**. Mr Rimpau had truly lied to them. But then why did he so openly admit the fact that his wife drove a grey Seat? If he'd known the significance of the car and it's colour in connection with the Green Meadows post office robbery, then he would never have admitted it. Now really! Tricky was an understatement! Following an impulse, Isy decided not to tell Amanda about Mrs Rimpau's grey Seat straight away. That wasn't exactly fair, but something inside her was desperately resisting **doing the dirty on** Mr Rimpau with this crucial piece of information.

---

prime suspect – Hauptverdächtiger; to lie through one's teeth – wie gedruckt lügen; to be down in the dumps – bedrückt sein; to do the dirty on sb – jmd. in die Pfanne hauen

It was more important to find Ruky first. Or the password for his computer. Or at least the girl with the blond pigtail. Before going to bed they **dawdled** around. The TV picture kept breaking up into flickering stripes, probably due to the bad weather, and neither of them was interested in watching a show which was continually being interrupted.

When they finally went to bed, Isy resolved to think about something nice, like her last birthday or next Christmas. But it just didn't work out. Every time she'd managed to conjure up a picture of her birthday or Christmas, Mr Rimpau's face or Ruky's sad, mocking smile and pretty lips forced their way into her dream and destroyed it. She had no other choice but to continue **brooding over** matters.

But at some point in the middle of the night, she must have fallen asleep, because when Amanda started tugging frantically at her arm, she had the feeling of waking up from an endless, deep sleep.

"There's somebody at the front door," whispered Amanda without a trace of being **flustered**. "We need the fake gun!"

"Give over!" mumbled Isy drowsily. "No one's going to break in again!"

"He's smaller than Mr Rimpau and fatter than Ruky," continued Amanda **undeterred**. "I watched him through the window in the hallway for a while. He sneaked around the house with a torch, but now

---

to dawdle – trödeln; to brood over sth – über etw. [nach]grübeln; flustered – aufgeregt; undeterred – unberührt

he's using a wire or something to **pick the lock**. You can hear it scratching."

It slowly dawned on Isy that Amanda was talking the truth. She'd obviously checked things out already. Maybe it was a real burglar breaking into the house.

"Shall we call the police?" she asked quietly.

"What for? We can deal with him ourselves!" said Amanda puffing herself up. "When he gets a blank up his backside he'll run like a rabbit!"

"There's always a first time for everything!"

It was really amazing how fear and terror had transformed the gentle Amanda this week.

Isy found Jelly Baby's shooter in the bottom drawer of the wardrobe. At the time all he'd wanted to do was save his own skin. He didn't care at all what would have happened if Trischi had found the gun in her bag. But maybe his nasty trick could help her out today.

A shame that Hagen Golz, otherwise known as Jelly Baby, couldn't see her now, creeping down the stairs behind Amanda, with his favourite toy in her hand.

Amanda immediately put her ear against the front door, but the scratching had stopped. They couldn't see the intruder through the window either.

Now it was Isy's turn to be sceptical. "Are you sure you saw someone?" she inquired cautiously.

---

to pick a lock – ein Schloss aufbrechen

"Couldn't it have been a branch blowing in the wind?"

"And how is a branch supposed to pick the front door lock?" hissed Amanda. "I definitely saw somebody! Like him over there! It *was* him!"

She pointed into the darkness outside. A **figure** was moving towards the house in the thin, dancing beam of light from a torch. It looked like the figure was carrying a huge object.

"I think he just **popped off** to get a ladder!" Amanda sounded worried. "Didn't we leave our bedroom window open?"

Yes, they had. Their bedroom window was slightly ajar. The guy breaking into the house had probably seen it. They'd give him an unforgettable greeting!

"Come on!" said Isy, giving a sign. Then they rushed up the stairs to their bedroom as quickly as the darkness would let them. They weren't a second too early. The intruder was already on the bottom **rung** of the ladder. They heard the ladder creak and saw a light shock of hair down below. Isy could feel Amanda's heavy breathing.

"Sh...sh...shoot!" whispered Amanda excitedly.

Yes, she was going to shoot. Hammer out a warning shot. Two at the most. That should be enough to **chase off** the intruder. She held Jelly Baby's revolver

---

figure – Gestalt; to pop off – verschwinden; rung – Sprosse; to chase off – vertreiben

as far out of the window into the cold autumnal night as she could, her hands trembling. Then she pulled the trigger. The gun's kick took Isy by surprise. Was that normal? And what about the blue flash which had bolted out of the steel **muzzle** at the same time as the blast? It looked terrifying! Did a fake gun always produce blank terror?

But before Isy could order her thoughts, they heard a muffled thud. It sounded like the intruder had fallen off the ladder. Horrified, Isy stared down into the darkness below.

"What now?" gasped Amanda. The shock seemed to have got more under her skin than she admitted. She'd turned ghostly **pale**. Her face would have made the perfect **advertisement** for cottage cheese.

"We have to go and take a look!"

"Not with me!"

"But maybe he hurt himself!"

"Then he shouldn't climb up ladders into other people's houses in the middle of the night!" Amanda was right, but Isy felt an **obligation** to help.

"Let's at least call the police!" Isy suggested.

Without waiting for Amanda to agree she turned on the light and went into the hall. She picked up the telephone and started to dial, but all she could hear was a *tut-tut-tut*. What now? Isy cautiously looked out of the window in the hall. The

---

muzzle – Mündung; pale – blass;
advertisement – Reklame/Werbung; obligation – Verpflichtung

intruder was lying near the front door, right in the middle of the yellow and auburn chrysanthemums. He couldn't have fallen from that high: he'd only climbed four or five rungs at the time of the shot.

"The telephone line's dead," she told Amanda, who was coming **tentatively** down the stairs. "Are you sure we shouldn't take a look? He's not moving at all!" Isy felt a strange sense of **dread**. He couldn't have seriously **injured** himself, could he?

To her astonishment, Amanda didn't try to hold her back when, after hesitating briefly, Isy opened the front door and peered out towards the stranger. On the contrary. Amanda pushed past her, picked the small torch up off the ground and shone it in his face.

"Be careful," Isy was about to warn her friend as Amanda spun around with a slight **shriek**.

"Isy, I think you shot Jelly Baby with his own revolver!" she stammered, before she sighed, fainted and fell down in slow motion next to the identified intruder, wearing no more than her yellow nightie.

---

tentative – vorsichtig/zögernd; dread – Furcht;
to injure – verletzen; shriek – (Angst-)Schrei

— 19 —

The following morning the three of them had breakfast together.

The mood at the breakfast table wasn't particularly good. The shock of the previous night was still **rattling their bones**.

What's more, Hagen Golz, the jelly baby fan, had **sprained** his right ankle in the fall, and Amanda had a headache. Isy, on the other hand, who'd had her hands full the previous night getting her classmate back on his feet with cold water and a few gentle slaps around the face, was still brooding over why **fate** had thrown the cheekiest and laziest member of the 6b into their nest. They could really have done without him!

And to make matters worse, he also had the appetite of a seven-headed **caterpillar**. Apparently he'd run away from home early the previous morning and had **hitch-hiked** all the way to Green Meadows. Of course, he'd thought the school lodge

---

to rattle one's bones – in den Knochen sitzen; to sprain – sich etw. verstauchen; fate – Schicksal; caterpillar – Raupe; to hitch-hike – per Anhalter fahren, trampen

was empty. He wouldn't forget the literally explosive welcome from his classmates Amanda and Isolde for the rest of his life.

He now also knew more about the extremely unpleasant **effects** of a fake gun. It gave them a gleam of hope that he might adopt less **repellent** hobbies in the future. But who could know for sure?

Hagen Golz had changed dramatically since the days when he had gone to the same kindergarten as Isy. Back then he used to celebrate carnival and name days dressed up as a peace-loving **toadstool**. Even his first days at school, when he was an average, somewhat shy classmate, seemed light-years away.

Nowadays hardly a lesson went by when he didn't attract attention either by his bad marks or his bad behaviour. Nor did a break-time pass by when he wasn't involved in a **brawl**.

He now sat enthroned between the two girls, quiet as a mouse, with breadcrumbs on his full lips. Every now and again he over-sensitively stroked his right ankle. They wouldn't even be able to count on his **brawn** to help them!

Amanda, who had just made a discreet inventory of their remaining food, fixed her eyes on Jelly Baby.

"We have to go shopping. Have you got any money?"

---

effect – Auswirkung; repellent – widerwärtig; toadstool – Pilz; brawl – Schlägerei; brawn – Muskelkraft

Hagen Golz blinked in bewilderment. He laboriously emptied his pockets. His revenue came to about ten Euros.

"We're not going to get very far with that!" said Amanda. "Did you at least bring some food with you?"

Jelly Baby nodded, relieved. Before he ran away from home he'd plundered the fridge thoroughly. He **limped** over to the boys' bedroom and brought his rucksack back for Amanda. She emptied its contents onto the table: crunchy sausages, cans, ham, a lump of Edam cheese and four packets of jelly babies. Then she packed away the treasures into the cupboard and warned Jelly Baby: "Just don't **get on your high horse** here!"

"I won't!" mumbled Jelly Baby, offended. He obviously still couldn't quite grasp that, of all people, he'd ended up with two girls from his class. The feeling was **mutual**. "Did you also run away?" he asked distrustfully.

"I wish we had! We've just spent the whole time cleaning this place up!"

Jelly Baby blinked in disbelief. "Cleaning?"

"Ask Isy!"

Isy tried to explain why they'd come to Green Meadows in a way that he could **grasp**, but in the end Jelly Baby didn't understand anything any more. "Are you stupid, or what?" Oh well, they

---

to limp – humpeln; to get on one's high horse – auf dem hohen Ross sitzen; mutual – gegenseitig; to grasp sth – etw. verstehen

were hardly expecting **a pat on the back** from him, either.

"And why did you run away?" asked Amanda persistently, but all she got was a blank look. If he was going say anything about what happened at home, then he certainly wouldn't tell this hot dog from Nuremberg. That was written all over his face.

Before they set off to the baker's, Isy made a **cold compress** out of a towel soaked in cold water and put it around Jelly Baby's ankle. It would do his foot good. Then she made it perfectly clear to him that he shouldn't let anyone into the house. Under absolutely no **circumstances**. If the worst came to the worst, he should threaten them with the police.

Jelly Baby sighed and rolled his eyes. He probably thought they were both suffering from **persecution mania**.

"Excuse me, but we're **embroiled in** a criminal case," Isy explained to him. "But it's a long story. For the time being, just do as we say, okay? So, don't let anyone in!"

Then Amanda and Isy went into the village. It was about time they were alone together.

"What did we do to deserve him?" cried Amanda, outraged. "He's just going to **get in our way**!"

That was the unfortunate truth. From now on

---

a pat on the back – Schulterklopfen; cold compress – kalter Wickel; circumstance – Umstand; persecution mania – Verfolgungswahn; to be embroiled in sth – in etw. verwickelt sein; to get in one's way – im Weg sein

the conditions to solve the 'Ruky case' would be much more difficult. If it was still at all possible.

Isy couldn't help feeling sorry for Jelly Baby nevertheless. She knew that he often had trouble with his parents. His father, who had been a professional officer in the GDR, had refused to slip into the uniform of the West German army after the Wall came down. He didn't want to be in 'the enemy's skin'. His wife was horrified by his decision, because she knew he'd pay for his honesty with unemployment. As a cook in a former **state establishment**, she then went about knocking on the doors of various personnel managers to try and get work. **To no avail**. The mutual **bitterness** in the family must have been really difficult for Jelly Baby and his two little brothers. Maybe he'd talk about it with her sometime, thought Isy. She just had to catch the right moment.

But first they headed for the baker's. This time the shop was pretty full. It wasn't only just before the weekend, the holidays were **coming to a close** as well. At any rate, the baker's wife didn't have any time to chat with the two girls. She only reminded them that the school's order for bread and rolls for the coming week had to be made by the next day at the latest.

"And how are we supposed to do that?" asked Amanda.

---

state establishment – staatliche Einrichtung; to no avail – vergeblich; bitterness – Groll; to come to a close – zu Ende gehen

"How many of you are there in the class?" asked the baker's wife.

"Thirty-one, plus a teacher," said Isy. "But some of them eat enough for three people!"

"That's fine by me!" laughed the woman behind the counter. Then she took two hot pieces of Danish pastry off the baking tray which had just been brought into the front room by a young girl, and added the pastries generously to Isy and Amanda's shopping.

"So, that's on me. Enjoy it!"

"Oh, thank you. That's very generous of you!" said Amanda, happy about the unexpected gift.

But Isy just stared at the girl who was leaving the front room with the tray. She was very pretty and had a **graceful** way of moving. Above all, she had a long, blond pigtail.

"Excuse me, I have to have a quick word with that girl!" she told the baker's wife urgently. "It's very important!"

If the baker's wife was surprised at Isy's sudden **request**, she didn't show it at all. "My daughter? Doren?"

She handed the girls their bags over the counter.

"Go around to the backyard. She'll be in the bakery!"

Doren, the girl with the pigtail, wasn't in the bakery. Straight after bringing the Danish pastries

---

graceful – anmutig; request – Bitte

into the front room, she'd jumped on her bike and was just about to leave the yard when Isy called out to her.

"Hey, can you tell us where we can find Ruky King?"

Doren's pretty face suddenly grew serious. She looked like the baker had baked her out of the softest pastry.

"How should I know?"

She knows, Isy thought in a flash. She's a worse **liar** than I am! She was obviously used to keeping a few secrets. How the baker's wife had **ranted on** about Ruky! She had to know how to keep a secret. If she didn't want to talk, Isy wouldn't **force** her either.

"Who are you anyway?" asked Doren irritably.

"Berliners!"

"Berliners? What kind of Berliners? East or West?"

"Central Berliners!" said Amanda, looking razor sharp.

"Look," said Isy softly, "it's just that we're worried about Ruky. He's disappeared without a trace since the party!"

Doren **squinted** as if she'd suddenly become **short-sighted**. "Since the party? What party?"

"A party for his **mates**."

---

liar – Lügner; to rant on – wettern über; to force sb – jmd. zwingen; to squint – blinzeln; short-sighted – kurzsichtig; mate – Kumpel

"And for us!" added Amanda proudly.

The girl laughed slightly. "You're wrong there. I'd have known about that!"

"We're not wrong!" insisted Amanda. "He ordered the Hermann Party Service especially for us!"

"Then you're even more wrong that I thought! Even if Ruky were a millionaire, he'd never order rubbish like that!"

She spoke as if she were Ruky King's personal advisor. Then she waved her hand casually and set off on her bike, turning the pedals so quickly that her long, blond pigtail bobbed up and down. Did Ruky really go for a **smug** cow like her!? S.O.S!

"Who is she anyway?" asked Amanda. "Do you know everybody in Green Meadows?"

"She's one of Ruky's friends. If you hadn't been polishing off the scrambled eggs at the time, then you'd have seen her standing at the fence the day before yesterday!" Isy frowned, lost in thought. "She's not as stupid as she **makes out**! She's probably on her way to him right now! At any rate, she's **up to her neck in it**!"

Amanda swung her string bag impatiently. "Oh, come on! Forget about the silly old cow! We still need to buy butter and eggs!"

They went to the supermarket, where two

---

smug – eingebildet, selbstgefällig; to make out – vortäuschen, sich hinstellen; to be up to one's neck in sth – bis zum Hals in etw. stecken

women in the wine section were talking about whether it was easier to get corks out of red or white wine bottles. They were of differing opinion.

There was a debate going in front of the cheese counter as well. One of the customers seemed to be complaining that there was too much choice. "Thirty-seven different cheeses!" he **grumbled**, looking around for people who shared his opinion. "Why on earth would anyone need thirty-seven different types of cheese? That's modern times for you!"

"Excuse me, sir," said a customer who was testing the softness of a **goat's** cheese with his thumb. "Do you remember how many types of beer used to be **available** in the GDR? I mean, with no connections?"

The man who had been complaining thought about the question for a few seconds. "Two?"

"I think you've hit the nail on the head," said the man with the goat's cheese in his hand politely. "And do you know how many types of beer the ancient Sumerians used to make three thousand years ago? No? Then let me tell you: exactly sixty types of beer. That's official. As you can see, sir, people's **demands** aren't down to modern times alone. Or were the two types of beer enough for you?"

"Thanks for the information!" said Amanda spontaneously as she put a lump of butter in her

---

to grumble – meckern; goat – Ziege; available – verfügbar; demand – Anspruch/Anforderung basket. "My dad will be amazed!" And turning to Isy she declared: "The old Sumerians discovered mathematics. They were capable of anything!"

On the way home they tested each other on **capital cities**.

As Isy tried **to take** Amanda **for a ride** with the capital of Australia, they both snorted with laughter.

"Changing the subject," said Isy as she got her breath back and the sturdy roof of the lodge came into view ahead of them. "Do you think it would be smarter to tell Jelly Baby about our **case** or not?"

---

capital city – Hauptstadt; to take sb for a ride – jmd. reinlegen/übers Ohr hauen; case – Fall

— 20 —

Jelly Baby was still sitting in the same place when they came home. He claimed, however, that he had changed the compress several times. His ankle was actually looking a bit better.

"Was anyone here?" asked Amanda.

Jelly Baby shook his blond hair. He'd **shaved** it all **off** last autumn and it had grown astonishingly quickly, but his ears probably got too cold in wintertime.

"Someone called though," said Jelly Baby while chewing on a few small, yellow jelly babies. "Wrong number!"

The girls looked at each other knowingly.

"Wrong number? Not likely!" scoffed Isy scornfully. "It's just a trick to find out if someone was at home! This guy's a shocker!"

"What guy?" asked Jelly Baby.

"You don't know him," replied Amanda. "We'll tell you about it later. Maybe."

Then she shoved a bowl of potatoes over the table to him. "Here. You can peel the potatoes!"

---

to shave off – abrasieren

Without a word of protest, Hagen Golz, the **dunce** of 6b, set about Amanda's command. He couldn't afford to be **defiant** in his situation. And maybe he peeled potatoes more often than they thought.

Meanwhile the girls set about cleaning the windows on the ground floor, but after a short time Amanda had to take a break.

"Phew!" she groaned. "You're setting a fast **pace** today, Isy! It's worse than my ballet lessons in Nuremberg!"

"What?" said Isy, gobsmacked. "You used to have ballet lessons?" Amanda had never even mentioned that before.

"Not for very long," Amanda admitted, "but at least I got to wear a tutu!"

"A what?" asked Isy and Jelly Baby simultaneously.

"You know, one of those white, fluffy ballet skirts." Amanda rolled her eyes in enraptured **recollection**. "It looked great!"

"I can imagine," grinned Jelly Baby disrespectfully. "Amanda Bornstein, the dancing **cauliflower**!"

Although that was a particularly nasty thing to say, even Isy couldn't help bursting into laughter. When she saw Amanda's upper lip wobble, she stopped laughing straightaway. It wasn't fair to

---

dunce – Schlusslicht; defiant – aufmüpfig; pace – Tempo; recollection – Erinnerung; cauliflower – Blumenkohl

make fun of her friend. Okay, she was pretty **chubby**, and it was hard to imagine her dancing on her tiptoes, but Isy was sure she didn't really look like a dancing cauliflower.

Fortunately, just then a dove-sized, cinnamon-coloured bird with blue wings landed on a bare branch near the kitchen window and craned its neck up and down.

"There he is again!" said Isy excitedly. "He was in the garden recently. Do you think he's escaped from somewhere?"

"It's just a **jay**," mumbled Jelly Baby after casting a brief glance at the stranger. "No reason to get excited. You find them wherever there are **acorns**."

"Strange. And I could have sworn he came from Schurpurmadraskeninkongheli!" said Isy, convinced. Surprising how natural the word sounded when she said it.

"Where?" said Amanda frowning. "Are you out of your mind? Where's that supposed to be?"

"No idea! Maybe I just dreamed it." That sometimes happened to her. Particularly in geography. Isy went back to work with a shrug of her shoulders.

As she rubbed her cloth over the window panes, she couldn't help thinking of Doren. What did Doren mean when she said, even if Ruky were a millionaire, he wouldn't have ordered a party ser-

---

to make fun of sb – sich über jmd. lustig machen;
chubby – pummelig; jay – Eichelhäher; acorn – Eichel

vice? Oh man, what was going to happen next! Was everything just a terrible mistake? At the end of it all would they have to pay for the blasted 'fireplace feast' out of their own pocket money?

If only she hadn't listened to Amanda in the first place! She'd had a strange feeling right **from the word go**!

Once the windows in the basement were sparkling like a window cleaner advertisement, Amanda swore never to go on holiday with Isy ever again. She was completely **drained**. She downed two bottles of Fanta.

"What about the curtains?" asked Isy.

"What curtains?" **groaned** Amanda. "Curtains are out!"

"But they have some here. Really nice, bright lace ones."

Isy had spotted a pile of curtains in front of the washing machine in the laundry. Give or take Amanda's taste, the curtains would stop the tall windows in the dining and recreation rooms from looking like plucked chickens.

"We just need to put them in the washing machine!"

"Then do it!" said Amanda **snottily**. "I've never used a washing machine in my life, and I'm not in a hurry to be in the *Guinness Book of Records* either!"

---

from the word go – von Anfang an; drained – erschöpft;
to groan – stöhnen; snottily – patzig

Then she shuffled into the kitchen to try her first potato soup. Isy heard her mumble her favourite phrase: "Ça suffit!" Then she went into the cellar and started **tinkering around** with the washing machine. She tried various buttons, but the machine refused to work. This was definitely a case for the class mothers. They'd have known how to sort this out, even if one of them had volunteered to climb inside!

After several more **futile** attempts she gave up. Amanda's potato soup was no real **consolation** for her **thwarted** ambition. She thought it had turned out a bit too thin.

Isy immediately thought of the joke about the recipe for Scottish tomato soup which her father liked to tell whenever he got the opportunity. It went: take a red coloured bowl and fill it to the brim with hot water! Of course, she resisted repeating the joke now. Amanda couldn't take any more **blows below the belt**. Besides, she'd only just started her new career as a cook.

But Jelly Baby seemed to still be a bit hungry after the silent meal. Full of hope he limped over to the fridge and came back with a bowl of frozen spaghetti.

"Hey, how about a bit of this? We can just warm up the noodles!"

---

to tinker around – herumfummeln; futile – vergeblich/sinnlos; consolation – Trost; to thwart – durchkreuzen; blow below the belt – Tiefschlag

"Have you never seen criminal evidence before?!" asked Amanda in a friendly tone.

"I heard wool was bad for the **digestion**!" Isy remarked.

Jelly Baby just stared at the frozen spaghetti. Were the girls off their rockers? Why were they talking such a load of rubbish? Why shouldn't they just **chuck** the spaghetti into a saucepan?

"Right this very second you are holding in your hands the key evidence to the robbery at the post office," said Isy solemnly. "Under those innocent looking noodles is a black woolly hat. We froze it so that no one would find it. Cool idea, huh?"

"Cool idea!" agreed Jelly Baby, dumbfounded. He seemed **to be** a bit **green around the gills**. "Did you really rob the post office or is that just another one of your calamity stories?"

"What makes you think *we* did it?" asked Amanda, outraged. "There's a whole load of other people mixed up in this! Like the writer of thrillers who's going to give us a reading next week, and a guy called Ruky, who nicks Seats and plays Mozart to his vegetables."

"I think the soup's **kicking in**!" groaned Jelly Baby and **rushed** to the boys' toilets as quickly as his swollen ankle could carry him, his hands pressed against his stomach.

---

digestion – Verdauung; to chuck – schmeißen; to be green around the gills – grün im Gesicht sein; to kick in – durchschlagen/wirken; to rush – sich beeilen

"Well what about that!" said Amanda, staring in amazement at Jelly Baby as he rushed off. "For the first time ever he gets the chance to prove what a lad he is, and he's already **pooing in his pants**! What a **wet blanket**!"

"Maybe what we told him really does sound a bit crazy!" said Isy self-critically. "Don't forget Hagen hasn't got much imagination."

"Thinking that we'd be capable of robbing a post office is bad enough!" grumbled Amanda. "We can forget about him!"

"Then we'll have to find Ruky on our own," decided Isy. It probably wouldn't have been a good idea to involve a weak character like Jelly Baby in a high-risk operation like this anyway. "I suggest we **stake out** Mr Rimpau's house."

"We do what?!" gasped Amanda.

"We check his house out this evening!" said Isy.

"In the dark? Are you out of your mind?"

"At least no one will see us then!"

"And how do we get there?"

"Easy. On foot. We can take Jelly Baby's torch with us."

"I'll be scared!" insisted Amanda.

"Just pretend we're taking a night-walk. You like night-walks, don't you?"

Yes, she liked night-walks. But all alone with

---

to poo in the pants – in die Hose machen; wet blanket – Weichei; to stake sb/sth out – jmd./etw. überwachen

Isy? It really was a shame that Jelly Baby was such a **wimp**.

"Alright then," Amanda finally agreed. "But I'm not going to take a single step if there's **fog**!"

"There won't be any fog," promised Isy. "There was nothing about fog in the weather forecast."

That same evening, after they'd made some excuse about popping out for some fresh air, they set off, armed with Jelly Baby's torch. The fog around the old lodge was as thick as **pea soup**.

---

wimp – Schlappschwanz/Waschlappen; fog – Nebel; pea soup – Erbsensuppe

– 21 –

"You took me for a ride!" puffed Amanda as she **frantically** tried not to lose Isy on the narrow path between the road and the wood.

Isy strode on, **unwavering** in the dancing light of Jelly Baby's torch.

My God, Amanda should be happy about the fog! It was a gift from above! They couldn't be better **camouflaged** for their operation.

Okay, the fog had its bad side, too. The mist didn't just make **visibility** a problem, it also meant they couldn't hear the **approaching** cars, so they had to be twice as careful.

The fog also blurred the outlines of things around them and made them look bigger. After a few minutes Amanda refused to continue because she thought a man was standing in the middle of the path, lying in wait for them.

"That's not a person. That's a bush!"

"And how do you know?"

"Oh, we've seen that a lot. My mum once

---

frantic – krampfhaft; unwavering– unbeirrt; camouflaged – getarnt; visibility – Sichtweite; to approach – herannahen

thought she saw two **dodgy** characters coming out of the woods and my dad armed himself with a big stick. But it turned out to be two perfectly normal **juniper** trees on the side of the path, puffed up by the fog."

Amanda wasn't sure whether Isy actually believed what she said, but as they got closer to the cause of her fear, she was relieved to see that her friend was right and the supposed monster was just a harmless bush.

Yet the fog seemed to be getting thicker all the time. After a good quarter of an hour they reached the neighbouring village of Bollwitz. There the fog was so thick that Isy started asking **passers-by** where she could find the writer's rented summer house.

Only the third person, a cyclist who **emerged** from the milky autumn evening under a street lamp, could give them information. He pointed them in a direction which was easier to guess than to see, and assured them: "Not more than fifty yards! It's the house with the low fence." Then he straightened his bobble hat and sang the praises of Mr Rimpau's books. "Exciting, well written, you have to give it to him. I used to buy the odd book by him. Nowadays I'd have to rob a bank to afford one!"

"And what about a post office?" asked Isy.

---

dodgy – zwielichtig; juniper – Wacholder;
to emerge – auftauchen; passer-by – Passant

"Not a bad idea!" Two blue eyes flashed at her, amused, before the fog **swallowed** the man and his smile.

"Everybody around here just complains about money!" observed Amanda, annoyed. "I thought it was all much more expensive over here before?"

She blew her nose noisily.

"Do you know how many packets we always used to send to the East? With chocolate, soap, coffee and clothes! We even gave my uncle a car!"

"We got chocolate, soap, coffee and clothes from my aunt in Bremen," nodded Isy. "They used to be really expensive over here. We couldn't afford a car. But books were cheap. And **rent**, too." She thought for a second. "Water and electricity are more expensive now. My mum almost hits the roof when we spend too long under the shower or leave the light on. It never used to **bother** her before."

"But on the other hand you can travel wherever you want now!" observed Amanda. That was true. If they ever had enough money then they wanted to travel through Canada by caravan. That was her dad's dream: having breakfast in the middle of the wild mountains and looking over the brim of the cup of coffee to enjoy the sight of a **moose** passing by in front of the window.

They tramped off doggedly in the direction that the man with the black bobble hat had indicated and

---

to swallow – verschlucken; rent – Miete;
to bother – stören/ kümmern; moose – Elch

tried to find the writer's weekend house from among the others which now and again loomed out of the mist.

"We don't even need to bother where there isn't a light on," Isy declared, when suddenly a dog jumped up next to her. He was greyer than all the fog put together and **grunted** cheerfully. "Hey, Alfredo!" she whispered in surprise. Then she bent over the low fence to tickle the dog's head. "So here you are!" She'd completely forgotten Alfredo. What a stroke of luck that he'd recognised her and not barked.

She cautiously tried the handle of the garden gate and when it opened she waved impatiently to Amanda to follow her.

Amanda pulled a face as if Isy had asked her to jump into an **abyss** of snakes. She crept into the garden reluctantly. What on earth was Isy thinking of now? What if the owner of the house suddenly took a look out of his window and spotted them both in his garden? What if the dog with the funny name gave away their **presence**?

She anxiously tried to give her friend a sign, but Isy wasn't even thinking of turning around. Instead she just followed the happily skipping Alfredo to a flat-roofed **log cabin**, which slowly began to emerge out of the soup of fog in front of them. The front door was bathed in the warm light of a lantern.

---

to grunt – brummen; abyss – Abgrund; presence – Anwesenheit; log cabin – Blockhaus

"Let's get out of here!" whispered Amanda, frightened.

But Isy grabbed her friend's cold hand and pulled her around the windowless side of the house to the rear. She'd guessed right: in front of them they had the perfect view of Mr Rimpau, enjoying his peaceful evening behind a large, **uncluttered** window.

The 'Wanted Man' was sitting on the sofa, surrounded by shelves of books and pictures. Nearby was a cosy log fire. It looked like he was watching a television somewhere in the corner of the room.

Amanda doubted Mr Rimpau was the only person in Germany doing that at the time. There was really no need to have fought their way through the night and the fog all the way over to this **godforsaken hole** Bollwitz just to find that out! Disappointed, Amanda **pleaded for** a **retreat**.

Their TV was waiting for them back at the lodge, too. There was a film on tonight with Julia Roberts, about some mythical pizza. Maybe they'd even pick up the recipe as they watched?

But Isy seemed to have taken roots in Mr Rimpau's garden. She stared **spellbound** into the living room without an **inkling** of shame. What was she waiting for? What, for goodness sake, needed to happen for her to abandon her **lookout**?

---

uncluttered – frei; godforsaken hole – gottverlassenes Nest; to plead for – flehen um; retreat – Rückzug; spellbound – gebannt; inkling – Hauch, Ahnung; lookout – Beobachtungsposten

"Come on!" hissed Amanda. "He's only watching television! Did we trudge all the way over here to see this?"

"I want to know if he's hiding Ruky!"

"And how do you intend to find that out?"

Good question. How did she intend to find that out? Isy shrugged her shoulders. There was no straight answer to that question. Lie in wait. Linger watchfully. Keep their eyes open. Stake him out. Whatever happened, she was going to stay put here until some clue came up. Like if Mr Rimpau got up from the sofa with a plate full of bread and butter and went down to the cellar to feed his **hostage**.

But he was sitting on the sofa happily watching television.

"I'll have a sore throat again tomorrow!" grumbled Amanda feebly.

She probably wasn't exaggerating. It made Isy feel uneasy the way the damp cold was seeping into her clothes. Her feet were already as cold as ice.

But eventually fate seemed to show some consideration. Mr Rimpau got up and **stretched**. Then the writer bent down and picked something up off the floor. Only when Isy looked more closely could she tell it was a cat. She was bigger and furrier than Selma. It was probably a **tomcat**. Mr Rimpau put the cat on his **lap** as he sat back down to continue

---

hostage – Geisel; to stretch – sich recken; tomcat – Kater; lap – Schoß

watching television. A peaceful image. An idyllic sight. Amanda yawned provocatively.

Okay, Amanda won. Isy had to admit she'd **messed up**. Mr Rimpau was a harmless man. Even if a few facts spoke against it, he'd never do anything as cruel as kidnapping Ruky. But it was important that she had seen it with her own eyes. Breathing a sigh of relief she gave the signal to go home.

Alfredo was surprised to see the girls leaving and he accompanied them on their way out. Isy stopped in front of the front door for a moment. The small, cast-iron lantern looked so inviting. It would be so nice if they could knock and be invited in. A cup of tea and a chat with Mr Rimpau would warm them up and be so pleasant. Instead of that they had to **sneak off** like thieves! Amanda looked like she was thinking exactly the same.

There was a light shimmering behind one of the two shuttered windows next to the front door. It was probably in Mr Rimpau's **study**, a kind of **monk's cell** where he could concentrate on his ideas and put them down on paper better than in the large living room, full of distractions. He probably kept his **typewriter** there as well.

Isy stepped up to the shutters full of curiosity. She had to put her face up close to the wood and

---

to mess up – verpfuschen/vermasseln/scheitern;
to sneak off – davonschleichen; study – Arbeitszimmer;
monk's cell – Mönchszelle; typewriter – Schreibmaschine

look through a **gap** which had warped with the damp to be able to see into the writer's workshop. It was just as she had imagined. The typewriter was an old machine, like the ones you saw in the movies, not some modern computer with all the **refinements**. He probably had one of those in his city apartment. At any rate, he didn't seem to care less about his electricity bill. Why was the desk light on when no one was in the room? Or was something lying on the couch next to the desk? Isy pressed her face so close to the wood that it hurt. She'd guessed right.

On a narrow sofa, his face to the wall, laid a figure in a green herringbone pullover with long, black hair. He was lying strangely still. He might have been asleep. But it was equally possible he was drugged or **sedated** with tablets.

For a fraction of a second Isy thought her heart stood still. Oh, **cripes**! Mr Rimpau really had locked up Ruky! What on earth were they going to do now?

---

gap – Spalt; refinement – Finesse; sedated – ruhig gestellt; cripes! – verdammt!

– 22 –

Neither of the girls could sleep that night. Amanda was the first to get up. She went into the kitchen to eat a cheese sandwich. Then Isy got up to make a **sketch** of Mr Rimpau's property. She drew the log cabin with all its windows and sketched a cross to mark the writer's study.

That would help the police **set** Ruky **free from** the writer's **clutches** in the morning.

Isy drew slowly and precisely. She had the feeling she was racked by hayfever, flu and **measles** all at the same time. She hadn't felt so down for a long time. Her disappointment with Mr Rimpau was higher than the Alps and deeper than the ocean.

Above all she felt **guilty**. If she hadn't kept the fact that Mr Rimpau's wife owned a Seat a secret from Amanda yesterday, then they would probably have been in touch with the police by now. Instead of that they'd **shielded** Alfredo's master! Most of all she felt sorry for the dog!

---

sketch – Skizze; to set sb free from sb's clutches – jmd. aus jmds. Klauen befreien; measles – Masern; guilty – schuldig; to shield sb – jmd. beschützen

"Do you think they'll **raid** the house?" asked Amanda as she looked over Isy's shoulder while she was drawing. She felt really sorry for her friend. The way Isy had **gone into raptures** about Mr Rimpau.

"Maybe they'll just **arrest** him!" said Isy full of hope. "I don't think he'll try to resist." Then she went back to bed. Amanda also crawled back to the top bunk.

For a while they listened to each other's breathing. They both wondered if the other had already fallen asleep, but there was no gentle regularity which might betray the peaceful sleeper. They were far too **worked up**.

"How about some liver sausage?" asked Amanda all of a sudden. "I can make you a sandwich if you want. Liver sausage is always good for the nerves!"

"Give me a break with your liver sausage!" groaned Isy, rolling over onto the other side.

As the night went on the fog seemed to thin out. The moon, which all of a sudden was hanging in front of their bedroom window like a slice of red orange, cast a shimmering beam of light onto the floor in front of their beds. When Isy was small, she often used to imagine walking along a long, lonely beam of light like this one, like a bridge to the stars. From time to time they seemed to be within her very reach.

---

to raid – stürmen; to go into raptures – ins Schwärmen geraten; arrest sb – jmd. verhaften; to be worked up – aufgeregt sein

"I keep having to think of Mr Rimpau!" sighed Amanda from the top bunk bed. "How did Ruky manage to get Mr Rimpau into trouble? Mr Rimpau doesn't even drive a grey Seat!"

Then she slipped down past Isy and landed on the floor with a bang.

"Are you hungry again?" asked Isy bad temperedly. "Don't be surprised if your jeans are too **tight**!"

"My jeans aren't too tight!" Amanda felt her way to the door and turned on the light. "I just want to **water** Aeschylus. I forgot all about him with this stress going on."

Isy watched Amanda through the open door. She took a **watering can** from the window sill and went over to her cactus. Then Isy also got up and went into the corridor.

"Isn't it a fine **specimen**?" asked Amanda lovingly. "When Ruky's back I'm going to ask him what music he'd recommend for Aeschylus."

"Amanda, I know who drives a grey Seat!" exploded Isy with her confession. "Mr Rimpau's wife! He told me yesterday himself, when you were getting your autograph book from our room."

Amanda's index finger, which was just about to loosen up the earth around the ball-headed, thorny cactus, froze in the air.

"And you only mention that *now*?"

---

tight – eng; to water – gießen; watering can – Gießkanne; specimen – Expemplar

Disappointment seemed to waft through the cool corridor.

"Then Ruky could have been free ages ago?"

Isy nodded, **overcome with remorse**.

"Suppose I'd done that to you?!" hissed Amanda, as if she only now grasped the **outrageousness** of holding back such important information. "You're some friend!"

Just then one of the doors opened and Jelly Baby appeared. He'd slipped his jeans on and was yawning. "Do you always talk so loud in the corridor?"

"Get lost!" hissed Amanda. "You're all we need right now!"

"No, wait!" said Isy. "Right now is exactly when we need you!" Then she turned to Amanda. "If Jelly Baby could help us out, then we wouldn't need to call the police," she said **beseechingly**. "Then we could settle things with Mr Rimpau ourselves."

"But I'm for calling the police!" insisted Amanda.

"Even if you mess things up for Ruky that way?"

"You just want to protect your beloved Mr Rimpau!" scoffed Amanda and snorted through her nose. But in the end she gave in.

"Then let's make a plan!" suggested Isy.

---

overcome with remorse – zerknirscht;
outrageousness – Ungeheuerlichkeit; beseechingly – bittend

They went back to their room where they offered Jelly Baby the neighbouring bed and slipped under their covers again. "Would you help us **put** a six foot, medium sized, not particularly muscular guy **out of action**?" was their first question to Jelly Baby.

He scratched his head thoughtfully. "Depends! Can he do karate?"

"No." Isy shook her head confidently. Karate and Mr Rimpau didn't seem to match. Then she told Jelly Baby the whole story. Maybe he was too tired to be surprised, but he listened to the series of **hair-raising** events without a trace of emotion.

"Why do you two want to **rescue** this Ruky guy?" he asked as Isy's report ended with Ruky's abduction to Mr Rimpau's summer house. "Do you both **fancy** him or what?"

Them? Fancy Ruky King? Outrageous! They looked into each other's **reddened** faces. Only Jelly Baby could be so stupid!

"Ever heard of something called solidarity?" asked Isy.

"We're not going **to leave** our mate **in the lurch**!" announced Amanda.

Then they started working out their plan. They thought carefully about each step, weighed

---

to put sb out of action – jmd. außer Gefecht setzen;
hair-raising – haarsträubend; to rescue – retten;
to fancy sb – auf jmd. stehen; to redden – erröten;
to leave sb in the lurch – jmd. hängen lassen

up the **pros and** the **cons**, and left nothing to **chance**.

"And what about Mr Rimpau's woolly hat?" asked Amanda.

"He has to promise to send it back to the post office anonymously!" Isy had already thought about that one.

By the time they'd worked everything out, it was four o'clock in the morning. Apart from New Year's Eve, Isy couldn't remember ever having stayed up so late.

"Shall we just go straight into breakfast?" asked Amanda enthusiastically. "We won't be able to sleep now anyway!"

Three minutes later she was snoring serenely on her pillow. Jelly Baby was also unusually still. His head had slipped a bit to the side and Isy could see that he'd also departed to the realm of dreams in the nearby bed.

Hey, they can't just do that to her, she thought as her eyes closed and she fell into a deep, soft, dark nothingness.

---

pros and cons – Für und Wider; chance – Zufall

– 23 –

By the time they woke up it was already that time of day when punctual people started peeling the potatoes for lunch.

"I reckon it's going to be pretty hot today!" said Jelly Baby as he sniffed the air after washing. "Smells of disaster!"

That was an extremely tactless thing to say in the presence of the two girls. It spoiled their already small appetite. But what were they supposed to do? He **was in on it** now! Besides, he'd smelled right. At breakfast they'd had a shock of the worst kind: Mr Rimpau was sitting in their recreation room with a smile on his face. Or to be more precise, he was sitting in the square box with the constantly flickering screen.

The writer was giving an interview to a **presenter** with carrot-coloured, curly hair about his new book, chatting away charmingly on some modern studio seating. It was amazing how nice and **sincere** he came across. No one would ever have

---

to be in on sth – über etwas Bescheid wissen;
presenter – Moderator; sincere – aufrichtig

thought he was capable of committing such a crime! Just as well they'd seen Ruky yesterday with their own eyes! – Isy took a deep breath. The unexpected **encounter** with the writer, who looked like a chocolate bar in his brown suit, gave them a great opportunity. Even Mr Rimpau couldn't be in two places at once. Maybe he wouldn't make it back from the Hamburg TV station before the evening? Then they could easily rescue Ruky from the empty house. If Isy were honest, she far preferred that idea, but the **end credits** destroyed the illusion. The interview with Mr Rimpau was a recording. The conversation had taken place a few days before. So they'd have to reckon with his presence in Bollwitz just as before.

The second surprise of the day turned up in a white BMW as they were just finishing their last 'official action' in the old lodge and were scrubbing the ground floor. It was a real disaster for Amanda.

"Help! My parents are here!" she screamed **thunderstruck**, dropping the scrubbing brush in horror. "What are they doing here?"

Before she went to greet them, she luckily thought of something more important.

"You have to hide Jelly Baby! If my parents see him, they'll think we've got twenty boys staying with us! They won't believe me that we've been here alone the whole time!"

---

encounter – Begegnung; end credits – Abspann;
thunderstruck – wie vom Donner gerührt

Then she went calmly into the garden **to give** a man with an arm in a plaster cast and a black moustache **a big hug**.

Isy watched through the hall window. Amanda's mother took a deep breath of healthy country air while Amanda's dad checked out the house in front of him **with the eye of an expert**. Then she dashed into the recreation room and, despite his protests, dragged Jelly Baby off. The **laundry** seemed to be a good idea. Amanda's parents were unlikely to look there.

She suggested he make himself comfortable on the pile of curtains until the air was clear again, but Jelly Baby just turned his nose up. Revolted, he shoved the curtains to one side with his one healthy foot. "Why don't you put them in the washing machine?"

"Because it doesn't work!" explained Isy with a shrug of her shoulders. Then she hurried back to the hall to say hello to Amanda's parents. They were already taking a look around, leaving dark traces of mud from the garden on the clean, damp floor.

"We just wanted to pop around to say hello because Mandi hadn't called us for a while," was her mother's **justification** for the **parental** check. She handed out some chocolate nuts in pink wrapping.

---

to give sb a hug – jmd. umarmen; with the eye of an expert – mit fachmännischem Blick; laundry – Waschküche; justification – Rechtfertigung; parental – elterlich

"Are you coping? Are you having some fun as well?"

Isy and Amanda grinned at each other knowingly. How could they best answer that? If they told the truth, Amanda's parents would pack her into the car and drive her home on the spot.

A deafening **clatter** and jangle in the cellar saved them from having to answer.

It sounded like someone was trying to blow up the house.

"That's... that's the washing machine," Isy explained, trying to sound believable. "It's really ancient!"

"The washing machine?" asked the Avon mother, astounded. "The things you two get up to!"

"Amanda's even learned to cook!" said Isy proudly. Then they showed their visitors their room and Isy watched the healthy arm of Amanda's father slipping an orange note into his daughter's trouser pocket.

Half an hour later it was all over. Amanda's parents roared off to a business dinner back in the capital. Amanda seemed to find the visit extremely embarrassing.

"Just turning up here like that!" she mumbled furiously as she carried a pile of magazines into the house, front page stories about the Royal Family which her mother had brought her in the car. "Sometimes I think they'll never grow up!"

---

clatter – Rattern

Then they went down to the cellar to **release** Jelly Baby.

It really was the washing machine which had made the terrible racket. With wide open eyes Isy saw the curtains spinning around in soapy water behind the thick glass of the porthole.

"Some people don't seem to realise that a washing machine needs electricity to run!" smirked Jelly Baby.

No electricity? Oh, right, the **plug**! Isy could see it too now. At home the plug was always in.

In any case Jelly Baby had succeeded in surprising them.

"And who's going to hang them up?" asked Amanda **peevishly**.

"It's not the end of the world!" grunted Jelly Baby scornfully. "If you want I'll even iron them for you."

"Really?" Amanda stared at Jelly Baby as if she'd never seen him before. "Why didn't you come earlier? There was loads to do here! Who would have thought you'd be such a good house-husband!"

"If all your parents ever did was argue and drink, then maybe you'd be one, too!" replied Jelly Baby. Then he limped back to the television and took the compress out of a bowl of cold water. The **swelling** had gone down a lot overnight, but they'd decided to keep treating the ankle until the evening.

---

to release – freilassen/erlösen; plug – Stecker;
peevishly – pikiert; swelling – Schwellung

It was important that Jelly Baby was in top form for Bollwitz.

Television and foot cooling, that was a **bearable lot**, and sometimes it looked like Amanda **envied** Jelly Baby's **sprain**. Isy kept thinking of things they had to do before Monday. First she did some dusting, though she hadn't thought of doing any dusting the whole time. Then she suggested hanging a 'welcome!' sign in the entrance hall and jollying up the rooms with ornate bunches of leaves. To give the place a really autumnal feel. No sooner was the greeting sign painted and the **foliage** collected from the garden than she thought of yet another new gag. But Amanda was neither willing nor capable of baking a gigantic gugelhupf for thirty-two people. And in her opinion, bedtime treats belonged on pillows in hotels, not in a grotty school lodge. Even if it was just a question of a dreary packet of cough sweets. There seemed to be a hotel manager hidden somewhere inside Isy. She just hadn't noticed it yet. After Amanda had successfully foiled all further **assassination** attempts by Isy, the moment she'd been dreading came: the hours had passed with autumnal slowness and the day had seemed to last for ever, but bit by bit, dusk was starting to fall over Green Meadows.

It was time for them to get ready for their operation in Bollwitz.

---

a bearable lot – ein ertragbares Los; to envy – beneiden; sprain – Verstauchung; foliage – Laub; assassination – Attentat

They slipped on their coats without saying a word and set off. It was just like the evening before, only there was no fog, and Amanda was carrying a small, white plastic bag. And of course Jelly Baby was new in the group.

When they reached Bollwitz, Isy, who had been restless all day, felt butterflies in her stomach, a feeling which she knew all too well from the dentist's waiting room. It was probably perfectly normal to be feeling nervous. After all she didn't raid a writer's house every day. But how else were they meant to free Ruky if they didn't want to involve the police? Oh, that Ruky! If only he hadn't been so stupid as to blackmail Mr Rimpau. Isy tried to calm herself down by taking deep breaths. In half an hour the whole nightmare would be over! And by tomorrow everything in Green Meadows would be back to normal.

Ruky King would be sitting back at his computer, or inspiring his pumpkins with Haydn, and the post office lady, Lilli, would be astonished to receive a parcel early on Monday morning with the woolly hat from the robbery in it. It was very clever the way the thriller writer **won** her **confidence** by tricking her with his books. Amanda and Isy had seen it with their own eyes.

The suspense grew **unbearable** over the last yards to Mr Rimpau's rented house. Would Alfredo

---

to win sb's confidence – jmds. Vertrauen gewinnen;
unbearable – unerträglich

be strolling through the garden again, or would he be in the house?

It would be easier to carry out the plan if he was in the garden. If he was inside the house, then Plan B would come into operation. Isy had the task of **luring** Alfredo out of the sitting room under some pretext and locking him up in another room, so that he couldn't help his master. Isy hated the idea of betraying Alfredo's trust. She hoped the dog would jump up to the fence right now. But she couldn't see him anywhere.

They went through the key points of their plan, whispering.

"Just so you know: I'm doing this for you, not for the **foreigner**!" grunted Jelly Baby and spat into the sand.

"What foreigner are you talking about?" asked Isy amazed.

"Ruky is born here and is about as foreign as you are!" murmured Amanda. Then she took off her Palestinian scarf and pressed it into Jelly Baby's hand. It was long enough to tie up Mr Rimpau's hands.

"Swear you won't **bottle out**!" whispered Isy. "Freedom for Ruky!"

"Freedom for Ruky!" swore Amanda. Her lips were trembling, and it looked like her feelings were about to **overwhelm** her. Jelly Baby wouldn't give

---

to lure – locken; foreigner – Ausländer; to bottle out – kalte Füße kriegen; to overwhelm – überwältigen

his word. He turned up his nose and looked at his watch. "In ten minutes then. Don't mess up!"

Then he tipped his hat and went down the road until he disappeared into the darkness. They were alone again.

"He's not really such a bad guy," said Amanda quietly, and Isy wasn't sure if she meant Jelly Baby or Mr Rimpau.

Isy pushed open the garden gate and turned towards the house with a look of determination in her eyes. She saw the warm light of the small lantern flickering through the leaves of the old trees.

With the same determination she knocked on Mr Rimpau's door.

— 24 —

Was it really only a week since she first met Mr Rimpau smoking in the corridor of the train to Green Meadows with his nice dog? To Isy it felt like a lifetime ago. So much had happened since then. Other people didn't go through as much in years!

Now they were sitting on the comfy upholstered furniture in the pleasant sitting room of the small house, drinking instant hot chocolate which the master of the house had just made for them in the kitchen.

Mr Rimpau was drinking a coffee, but Isy had probably **spoilt** it for him by asking if they could take a look at the **Holy of Holies**, his study.

Mr Rimpau stirred his coffee slowly. Then he said they'd be horrified if he let them see the study. It was infamously untidy! He didn't want to set a bad example. What a **lying crook**!

Of course they'd be horrified. For sure. Not because of his untidiness, but because of what Mr

---

to spoil – verderben; Holy of Holies – das Allerheiligste;
lying crook – verlogener Schuft

Rimpau was hiding from them in his study: Ruky King to be precise! Oh, how she **despised** him!

"How's the house cleaning going?" asked Mr Rimpau, changing the subject. "Over the worst?"

"Pretty much, yes," sighed Amanda, "but you never know what Isy's going to think of next!"

"You two are absolute heroes!" said the writer charmingly and threw a fresh log of birch-wood onto the fire. "I might just write you both into my new book..."

"What? We're going to be in your next thriller?" cried Amanda delighted. "Did you hear that, Isy?" Amanda seemed **to be** utterly **beside herself**. She'd obviously completely forgotten that they were already playing a role in a thriller. Unfortunately a real one.

"Oh, it doesn't always have to be thriller," said Mr Rimpau mysteriously. "Does it, Alfredo?"

The dog, who was **dozing** near the warm fire, wagged its tail politely. Poor Alfredo. Isy looked at her watch. They'd have to lure him out of the room in two minutes.

"We're more comedy material anyway!" suggested Amanda. "Or for a family saga. With nobility and stuff." She paused for a moment. "Do you also think it's unfair the way the Royal Family is treating Princess Di at the moment?"

Sadly for Amanda the writer had no time to ex-

---

to despise – verachten; to be beside oneself – ganz aus dem Häuschen sein; to doze – dösen

press his opinion on the matter. Isy jumped to her feet and claimed the dog needed to go out. "Come on, Alfredo. Walkies!"

For a moment it looked like Mr Rimpau was about **to object** by pointing out that Alfredo was well trained enough to let them know if he had business to do, but the dog had already got up and was following Isy into the corridor.

It was a tiny corridor with three doors. The one to the kitchen was slightly ajar.

"Come on, dinner!" whispered Isy knowing perfectly well that the kitchen is any dog's favourite room. Alfredo **plodded** innocently into the **trap**. He had barely gone into the kitchen, sniffing the floor, when Isy quickly closed the door behind him. Phew, she'd made it! They were now safe from Alfredo.

Now all she had to do was open the front door and let in Jelly Baby. He had been lying in wait outside. As quiet as a mouse, he crept into the corridor, pressing himself against the wall like a secret agent. His coat smelt of the damp cool of the evening, and he was breathing quite quickly. He was probably really nervous, although he'd never admit it.

"Everything's going according to plan," Isy assured him quietly. "Wait for the signal!" Then she slipped back into the sitting room, not forgetting to leave the door slightly open. No one seemed to have missed her.

---

to object – Einspruch erheben; to plod – stapfen; trap – Falle

The flames in the fireplace crackled slightly, and Mr Rimpau and Amanda were talking about the Canary Islands. For two to three minutes Isy looked at the fire **wistfully**. What a shame! She'd never sat in front of a real fireplace before, and now there was no time to enjoy it. Everything was going according to plan and behind the door Jelly Baby was **longing** feverishly **for** some action. Isy suddenly put the white plastic bag, which Amanda had carried from Green Meadows to Bollwitz, onto the coffee table. Amanda had played her part magnificently up to now. No one could have chatted with their host as harmlessly as her. With a bit of luck she still knew what had to be done.

Amanda knew. She took the frozen bowl of out of the bag. It was misted up with defrosted water. She held it out to their host. "This is for you! We made it ourselves!"

Surprised, Mr Rimpau took the ice-cold present. "Oh, spaghetti!" he said, **baffled**.

"The real present is underneath the spaghetti," explained Isy. "You'll find it when you **thaw** the contents."

"It's something you've been looking for for a long time!" said Amanda mysteriously.

Mr Rimpau's expression **betrayed** the fact that he understood absolutely nothing.

Now the next phase of their plan could begin.

---

wistfully – wehmütig; to long for – sich sehnen nach;
baffled – verdutzt; to thaw – auftauen; to betray – verraten

Isy was supposed to go up to the big glass façade and pretend to look out for the dog. In reality her aim was to get Mr Rimpau out of his armchair and into a position where he was standing with his back to the door.

Only then could Amanda ask in a loud voice whether he had any jelly babies in the house, the cue for Jelly Baby to spring into action.

Strangely enough this also **went like clockwork**.

Isy commented about how long Alfredo had been outside and went up to the window where she pretended to look for the dog. When she pointed out that there was another, bigger dog than Alfredo in the garden, the writer came and stood next to her, staring out **anxiously** into the darkness. Someone else's dog in his garden? What was that?

"Do you happen to have any jelly babies in the house?" trumpeted Amanda loudly. After that everything happened really quickly.

With a speed they would never have thought possible for his size, Jelly Baby shot into the room and slipped his baseball cap over the surprised writer's face from behind. In a flash he pulled Mr Rimpau's arms to his back and tied them together with Amanda's favourite scarf. It was all so perfect. Things couldn't have worked out better in an episode of 'Miami Vice', 'Derrick', 'Simon and

---

to go like clockwork – wie am Schnürchen laufen;
anxiously – besorgt

Simon' or 'Columbo'. Isy had no regrets about getting Jelly Baby involved.

"What's going on?" asked Mr Rimpau, astonishingly calm. "I hope you know what you're doing!"

Then they led him, bound and **blindfolded**, back to his armchair.

For a moment there was an **oppressive** silence in the room.

Then Isy plucked up the courage to apologise on behalf of everybody for their unusual **behaviour**. "But it's your own fault!" she said bravely. "We know you're hiding Ruky! We even know you were in his house and looked through everything, although you told us you weren't even in Green Meadows that day! But we saw you with our own eyes!"

"How do you know?" asked Mr Rimpau coolly.

"Because we were hiding underneath the sofa," blurted out Amanda. "Isy recognised your chewed up shoes!"

"Ruky made a mistake trying to blackmail you!" continued Isy. "He'd recognised your wife's grey Seat. But he doesn't have the woolly hat which you've been looking for all over the place. We found it in the old secretaire in the school lodge. He'd hidden it there. And we froze it just **to be on the safe side**. It's in the bowl which we brought for you!"

"What an ice-cold idea!" said Mr Rimpau ad-

---

blindfolded – mit verbundenen Augen; oppressive – bedrückend; behaviour – Verhalten; to be on the safe side – vorsichtshalber miringly. His voice sounded a bit strange from under the baseball cap.

"We want to **swap** the woolly hat for Ruky!" said Isy firmly. "Do you agree?"

"I'll think about it!" replied Mr Rimpau after hesitating slightly.

"You don't **stand a chance**, man!" chipped in Jelly Baby. "Otherwise we'll hand you over to the police like a Christmas present!"

"Who's that?" asked Mr Rimpau, astounded. "How many more unknown visitors do I have?"

"That's Jelly Baby," said Amanda. "You're wearing his cap."

"He's from our class," explained Isy. "And he's right. We could have told the police about you ages ago! But because you were so nice to us, to Amanda and me, and because you're probably not such a bad guy, we thought we should sort it out among ourselves. The only **condition** is: you have to give the post office back what you stole. Anonymously for all we care!"

"Down to the last penny!" added Amanda.

"What other **options** do I have?" asked the writer politely.

"None!" said Isy resolutely.

"None!" repeated Jelly Baby and Amanda as if speaking from the same mouth.

"We'll only untie you once you've accepted our

---

to swap – tauschen; to stand a chance – eine Chance haben; condition – Bedingung; option – Möglichkeit

conditions and we've let Ruky King out of your study!"

"How do you know Ruky's here?"

"We watched your house yesterday evening!" said Amanda.

It looked like Mr Rimpau **slumped** a bit. Maybe his tied up arms were just uncomfortable.

"It looks like all the evidence is against me!" he said. "But I've got an idea!"

In a flash Mr Rimpau jumped up with all his **might**, knocking over the armchair. Isy **cowered back** to the door. Taken aback, Jelly Baby froze like a statue.

But not Amanda. Just as Mr Rimpau had managed to shake the baseball cap off his head, she reached into the plastic bag and took out a green, gleaming object which she threw at his head with all her might. Mr Rimpau **shrieked in pain** and fell to the floor.

Amanda looked at Aeschylus lovingly.

"He's much more humane and environmentally friendly than your fake gun, don't you think?" she asked Jelly Baby, who was **gaping at** her in astonishment. "And just as **effective**." She pointed at the writer lying on the floor.

Unbelievable! Amanda had brought her cactus

---

to slump – zusammensacken; with all one's might – mit aller Kraft; to cower back – ausweichen; to shriek in pain – vor Schmerzen schreien; to gape at sb – jmd. mit offenem Mund anstarren; effective – wirksam

with her?! Before Isy could really grasp what had happened in the last three seconds, the sitting room door flew open. On the **threshold** was Ruky King.

"You idiots!" he said furiously.

threshold – Türschwelle

— 25 —

What a disgrace! What a humiliation!

It wasn't exactly a winning team which **slunk off** back to Green Meadows. How on earth had they managed to make such fools of themselves? Something had gone very wrong, but they didn't know what. A doctor had come around to remove the seventeen cactus **thorns** from Mr Rimpau's face with **a pair of tweezers**. The writer hadn't even **deemed them worthy of another glance**.

After his dramatic entrance, Ruky, who could have **shed** some **light on** the matter, had disappeared as if he'd been swallowed up by the earth. Amanda said she saw a silhouette that looked like Ruky darting through the garden.

They had no other choice but to quickly stammer their apologies to their host, who was still being attended to by the doctor, and set off home without Jelly Baby's baseball cap. To make matters worse it was now bucketing down with rain.

---

to slink off – sich davonschleichen; thorn – Dorn; a pair of tweezers – eine Pinzette; to deem sb worthy of a glance – jmd. eines Blickes würdigen; to shed light on – Licht in etw. bringen

"Bloody weather!" grunted Jelly Baby who was **grieving for** his baseball cap. "You two really are the calamity queens!"

As if they could do anything about the weather! Nobody could ever have guessed that Ruky **was in league with** Mr Rimpau, either!

The question was: Why? Isy was dying to know. That and a few other things. Of course, she'd **got hold of the wrong end of the stick** completely. "A real mess!" was a major understatement. They wouldn't even exist for Mr Rimpau from now on. They'd have to live with that. But the case wasn't over yet! If the writer hadn't been keeping Ruky hostage, then what was he doing in his house? Was he letting him hide there from somebody? If so, from whom? Good question! And it was easy to answer as well: from the man whose black, frozen woolly hat Amanda was right now carrying back home to the fridge.

You could look at it any way you wanted: they still had the one and only piece of **corroborative evidence** for the robbery at the Green Meadows post office!

"I think we can still **solve** the robbery!" Isy interrupted the oppressive silence as they marched beneath the dripping trees along the country lane.

---

to grieve for – trauern um; to be in league with – unter einer Decke stecken; to get hold of the wrong end of the stick – sich schwer irren; corroborative evidence – eindeutiger/klarer Beweis; to solve – lösen

"What about if we go over to Ruky's right now and **give him the third degree**?"

"The party's over!" grunted Jelly Baby.

"He's right," said Amanda, agreeing with the **disheartened** hero of Bollwitz. "Besides, Ruky won't be at home."

"And if he is?" said Isy stubbornly. "He's the only person who can tell us what's really going on. And I think we deserve to finally know. We **put** our necks **on the line** for him!"

Her companions remained silent.

"We can just take a look to see if he's there! Quickly? Please, please!"

In the end she got what she wanted: they took a **lap of honour** to the Kings' house and it was exactly as Amanda had said. The house lay dark and silent in the equally dark and silent garden. Ruky hadn't come home yet.

That evening, when Amanda slipped into her yellow nightie, she told Isy, the wind, Jelly Baby, and all the hedgehogs, **midges** and twists of fate of Green Meadows: "If anyone disturbs me tonight, I'm going to **knock them senseless**!"

At thirty-two minutes past midnight Isy gave Amanda good reason to do so. "Hit me, if you want! I'm sorry, but I just had to wake you up!"

---

to give sb the third degree – jmd. in die Zange nehmen; disheartened – entmutigt; to put sth on the line – etwas riskieren; lap of honour – Ehrenrunde; midge – Mücke; to knock sb senseless – jmd. k.o. schlagen

Amanda seemed to rise out of a deep in bowl of apple sauce. She'd even forgotten about her knock-out-offer in her dreams. She couldn't grasp at all what Isy was saying. She slowly came around and mumbled: "Is... is someone in the cellar?"

"No one's in the cellar," whispered Isy. "It's all okay."

"So why did you wake me up?"

"Because you know how to handle a computer."

"But we don't have a computer here."

"I'm talking about Ruky's PC. I think I know the password!"

"What password?" yawned Amanda.

"Come on, wake up!" insisted Isy. "The password with five letters!"

"Couldn't this wait until tomorrow?"

"Unfortunately not. Ruky might be back home tomorrow. And he's unlikely to let us go **sniffing around** his computer!"

"You don't want to...?"

"That's right," said Isy guiltily. "Believe me. We have to do this. Otherwise we'll be stuck with the woolly hat until **Whitsun**! The **culprit** is in the computer!"

Isy turned on the light and threw Amanda her pullover.

"And what are we going to do with Jelly Baby?" asked Amanda.

---

to sniff around – herumschnüffeln; Whitsun – Pfingsten; culprit – Täter

"Nothing. Let him dream on!"

They crept out of the house and hurried up the now familiar High Street. There were very few lights on in the houses and the only people they met were a young couple who were wrapped up in themselves. At one point a cat scared them as it **bolted** out of a garden, and another time Amanda slipped on the wet leaves and almost fell down.

Soon they were in the King's garden, unlocking the front door quietly. Just as Isy was about to go into the veranda, Amanda grabbed her by the arm. "What if his mum's back?" she whispered.

"I doubt it!" Isy sniffed the air. It was old and **stale**. **What's more** it was cold in the house. It hadn't been heated for at least four days.

They felt their way through the veranda and the corridor, and as their eyes adjusted to the darkness, they cautiously went up the stairs. Only once they were in Ruky's room did they dare turn on a light after quickly closing the curtains. Amanda turned on the computer and rubbed her **numb** hands. If she ever told anyone the things she got up to at night in Green Meadows, they'd take her for Baron von Münchhausen's granddaughter.

"What's the password?" she asked her friend.

"Doren!"

"What? The blond girl with the pigtail? What makes you think that?"

---

to bolt – schnell rennen; stale – abgestanden;
what's more – außerdem; numb – klamm

"I don't know. Just a feeling." Isy laughed **mischievously**. "I think he likes her. My **gut-feeling** says she and the red-haired guy were there when the Seat was stolen. That's why Ruky's scared of the police. Not for himself. He wants to protect his mates." She stretched herself out on the carpet and watched the shadows on the **slanting** walls. "Can you imagine what the baker's wife would say? Her wonderful daughter is the Seat nicker's girlfriend! And Ruky King at that!"

"Okay! If you think so… I'll give it a try!"

It worked! As Amanda typed in the word 'Doren', a miracle happened. She'd **broken the code**! On the screen there was a text underneath the heading: SECRET!

"Hey, this is it!" cried Amanda breathlessly. "Take a look!"

"Really?" Isy jumped up and rushed over to Ruky's desk. Side by side they read Ruky's report about the robbery at the Green Meadows post office.

"And I shook his hand!" said Amanda, horrified.

"I don't believe it!" groaned Isy. "The Drake! And we ate his fireplace feast!" Then they looked at each other with wide open eyes. "We have to call the police!"

---

mischievously – verschmitzt; gut-feeling – gefühlsmäßige Ahnung; slanting – schräg; to break the code – das Passwort knacken

— 26 —

Jelly Baby heard the whole story the next morning at breakfast. He almost fell into his **cocoa** with surprise. The 'calamity queens' had solved the case on their own? In the middle of the night? On some guy's computer? In somebody else's house?

"The coolest thing was the police already knew!" Amanda explained, almost **insulted**. "After our visit to Mr Rimpau yesterday evening, Ruky **turned himself in** to the police. They told us on the phone."

"Ruky said he stole the grey Seat on his own, and all the other ones too, but we have our doubts there," threw in Isy. She winked over the kitchen table at Amanda.

They'd put Jelly Baby's delicious ham on the table and were eating hungrily.

"In any case, Ruky came up with the idea of blackmailing his masked friend pretty quickly. He went about it carefully. After all, he didn't **have a clean slate** himself. But he thought a little black-

---

cocoa – Kakao; insulted – beleidigt; to turn oneself in – sich stellen; to have a clean slate – eine weiße Weste haben

mail on the side wouldn't do any harm. Then he went to the street where he stole the Seat and took a look at the nameplate. Then he was in the know. He **hatched a plan** with his friends. They put two blackmail letters into the post box of the Seat owner, a certain Harry Hermann who happens to run a Party Service. They just wanted to make him nervous. Then they ordered a party dish from his company. They wanted Harry Hermann to bring the dish in his Seat, as final **proof**, rather than his usual delivery van. That's why they put the delivery van out of action. They wanted to sell Mr Hermann the black woolly hat when he came around."

"He admitted all that to the police?" asked Jelly Baby in disbelief.

"No way! That was all in his computer. The whole plan. Step by step," explained Amanda.

"The only problem was when he couldn't find the woolly hat in the old secretaire one day," continued Isy. "He couldn't even find it when he searched through our bedroom. By then his friends had got cold feet and wanted to pull out. They didn't want to be involved in the blackmailing. Ruky managed to persuade them to take out the delivery van. They put a **raw** potato in the **exhaust pipe**."

"Farmer's trick!" grinned Jelly Baby. "As old as the hills!"

"Still seems to be pretty effective though," said

---

to hatch a plan – einen Plan schmieden; proof – Beweis; raw – roh; exhaust pipe – Auspuff

Amanda with her mouth full. "Anyhow, Mr Hermann didn't turn up at Ruky's in the delivery van. We thought we were seeing things when he told us we could choose a party platter!"

"Of course Amanda chose the biggest one!" said Isy. "The amazing thing is she took it out of his car herself and didn't even notice it was a grey Seat!"

"You wouldn't have spotted it in the dark either!" said Amanda in her defence. "Besides, it didn't matter at the time."

"He seemed like a really nice guy at the time," recalled Isy. "His hair was really strange. Like a duck's tail. That's why we called him The Drake! Apart from that nothing seemed unusual about him at all."

"The strange thing was that Ruky didn't **turn up**. I mean, it was *his* party! But back then we didn't know that he'd offered the story to Mr Rimpau for his next book. Mr Rimpau was keeping him in Bollwitz because he was worried Harry Hermann might have **smelled a rat**," explained Amanda.

"Ruky told the police that Mr Rimpau had spent days trying to get him to go to the police and clear up the robbery at the Green Meadows post office," said Isy, ending the report.

Meanwhile Amanda had taken the spaghetti bowl out of the fridge. My goodness, they'd **carted**

---

to turn up – auftauchen; to smell a rat – Lunte riechen;
to cart sth around – etwas rumschleppen

it around the place over the last week! But this time it was for good. It truly was Spaghetti criminale!

"There's something else we have to do!" said Jelly Baby. "Are you coming with me?"

They took the midday bus and drove through the picture-book Mark Brandenburg countryside, washed clean by the previous night's rain. Soon they were in town. The police station was on the market square and they immediately asked for the **inspector**.

The police officer **on duty** spoke on the phone with his colleague and they were eventually led into a plain office with several green plants. A grey-haired man was sitting behind his desk. **Without beating about the bush**, Amanda put the frozen bowl down in front of him.

"Voilà! The mask from the Green Meadows post office robbery!" The man looked dumbfounded at the frozen noodles.

"I presume you are Isolde Schütze and Amanda Bornstein, who spoke with my colleagues last night, right?" he asked in a friendly manner and invited them to take a seat. "So, tell me everything!"

So they told him their story, and the inspector, who didn't look like a proper inspector at all, more like a Geography teacher, occasionally let a cheerful smile dart over his face.

He turned to the frozen bowl full of curiosity.

---

inspector – Kommissar; on duty – Dienst haben;
without beating about the bush – ohne Umschweife

"You just need to thaw the spaghetti, wash and dry the mask, and there's your evidence!" said Isy. "Was there any reward, by the way? It's just we had a few **expenses**. The fireplace feast from Hermann's party service, for example."

"It really wouldn't be right if the **bill** went to Mrs King, or even to us," Amanda continued with her well-practised look of innocence. "We only ate the dish **as a cover**. We were in the middle of our investigation, if you know what I mean."

The inspector knew what she meant. He promised to sort matters out, but there wasn't a reward as such. The **haul** at the post office had been too small. No one had suffered any major losses.

"Why did the man rob the post office in the first place?" asked Jelly Baby from somewhere behind a green plant. "He had enough to eat, didn't he?"

The inspector admitted that the first **cross-examination** during the night hadn't led to much. But it was usually always the same reason: "Too much credit, too many **debts**, and a lifestyle that's too extravagant," he said saddened. "And when they're up to their neck in it, they see on TV how to get a quick few thousand." Fortunately this didn't happen too often.

"And what's going to happen to Ruky now?" blurted out Amanda.

---

expenses – Auslagen; bill – Rechnung; as a cover – zur Tarnung; haul – Beute; cross-examination – Kreuzverhör; debts – Schulden

The inspector's reply sounded reassuring. Of course they'd have to take Ruky King in hand. He was still known as the Seat Nicker. But the fact that he'd turned himself in and helped the police clear up the robbery would be **taken** strongly **into consideration**.

"You should also take into consideration that he comes from a difficult background," added Isy. "His father's Cuban, and that's why some people have turned against him all of a sudden. The former GDR has become quite racist. It's hardly surprising that a guy like Ruky King **freaks out**, is it?"

Then they shook hands cordially, and the inspector accompanied them into the corridor.

"I hope I'm saying goodbye to two future colleagues!" he said charmingly, and two little **dimples** on his **cheeks** made him look like a real, shrewd TV inspector rather than a Geography teacher.

"That would suit him, wouldn't it!" said Amanda as they went down the stairs to the exit. "You and me as cops!"

"Why not?" thought Isy aloud. "Top jobs in the Criminal Investigation Department? They need women!"

"But not you two!" grunted Jelly Baby. "At the end of the day they're there to *stop* disasters, not make them happen!"

---

to take sth into consideration – etw. berücksichtigen;
to freak out – ausflippen; dimple – Grübchen; cheek – Wange

"Watch it!" snapped Amanda. "You'd be my first arrest. Who started that fire in the corridor anyway?"

Back on the street, they looked across the quiet, Sunday market square and saw a snack bar. The smell of **charcoal** and sausage fat drifted over to them and **tickled** their noses. As if on command, they rushed over to the snack bar together. They just had enough time for a hot dog before their bus came. Then they rolled back to Green Meadows with full stomachs, pleased with their day.

In the afternoon the girls washed their hair and Amanda tried out some red dye. The stuff came out of the tube like ketchup and they feared the worst, but the end product didn't look at all bad. The other girls in the class would be green with envy. Amanda was the kind of girl who could wear anything.

Then she buried herself in her magazines and caught up with the royal gossip, sighing with pleasure. When the whole of Year Six started **romping around** here tomorrow, she wouldn't have another opportunity.

Isy also tried to get back into her Parking Lot thriller novel. She hadn't had the book in her hand since the journey here. It was strange: the story didn't **grip** her anymore! She didn't care in the least if the killer was Mrs Sanders' son or not.

What interested her more than anything was

---

charcoal – Holzkohle; to tickle – kitzeln; to romp around – herumtollen; to grip – fesseln

what Mr Rimpau was looking for that day in Ruky's house. It was the only question in the Green Meadows criminal case which hadn't been cleared up. It was a shame they could never pop around to his house again. He'd never forgive them for what happened with Aeschylus. How on earth were they going to explain to Dr Trisch that the reading would no longer be taking place?

They discussed their plans for following day over dinner. Jelly Baby volunteered to pick up six **loaves** and a hundred and fifty rolls from the baker's. They'd be ready for the **onslaught**. After that the girls would have to discuss the rest of the shopping with Trischi.

It was a strange feeling to think it was their last evening alone in the old forester's lodge. With it a week of unforgettable holidays were coming to an end. Each of them felt wistful and relieved at the same time.

Isy decided to say something really nice to Amanda at the end of their time together.

As Amanda's bare feet passed **blissfully** by her pillow to the top bunk after an oily romantic movie made in Italy, she told her what a great friend she was. Through thick and thin, dust and filth.

"Amanda," said Isy solemnly. "If you **consent**, I would hereby like to name you an Honorary East German!"

---

loaf – Brotlaib; onslaught – Ansturm; blissfully – selig; to consent – zustimmen

Unfortunately Amanda didn't reply. She had fallen asleep during the **awards ceremony**. Up until now, nights at the school lodge had been pretty busy. Isy also snuggled up under her covers and tried to recover at least a little of her lost sleep. They **slept like logs**.

They slept and slept and slept, and were still sleeping when somebody started knocking **persistently** at the front door and a loud babble of voices drifted up to their bedroom from the garden.

Only when someone somewhere called Dr Trisch's name did they wake up, startled. What on earth was going on? What was that terrible **racket** in front of the house?

"We've overslept," announced Jelly Baby sheepishly from the corridor. "It's already eleven o'clock. The others are outside. I'll let them in!"

Good heavens! Was their class there already?

The sign! thought Isy, horrified. They hadn't pinned up the 'welcome' sign yet.

The very next moment the house started shaking from the commotion. Year Six stormed into all the rooms, up the stairs and into their bedroom.

"Hey, look at that! They're still asleep!" yelled Ingo and Karsten and were pushed aside by a few girls. All of a sudden Saskia and Binette, Liane, Jennifer and Sophie were standing in front of their bed, laughing and chatting away.

---

awards ceremony – Verleihung; to sleep like a log – wie die Steine schlafen; persistent – hartnäckig; racket – Krach

"Hey, you **lazybones**, get up! The holidays are over!" cried Binette cheerfully.

Saskia, who was as brown as a honey bee, threw open the window. "This place is paradise! It's so quiet! And it's for free!" She turned to the girls with a **reproachful** expression on her face. "We paid two thousand Euros for Tenerife and couldn't even get a decent night's sleep! We had to make up for it on the beach."

With a twinkle in her eyes Liane asked them how they'd come up with the mad idea of cleaning the lodge. Jennifer Niemann turned up her nose as usual.

"There's nothing going on in this dump!" She shuddered at the thought and gave Isy and Amanda a **compassionate** look. "You poor things! I can tell that you've been bored out of your minds here!"

---

lazybone – Faulpelz; reproachful – vorwurfsvoll; compassionate – mitleidig

— 27 —

At some point in the early evening of the following Thursday, a red Golf stopped in front of the school lodge.

A man got out who was not tall, but not small either, not particularly strong, but not at all **weedy**. There were two plasters on his forehead and he had a friendly smile on his face.

"My name's Mr Rimpau," he told the pupils who stood around gaping at him. "If you'd like, I can do my reading now!"

And that's exactly what happened.

In no time at all they cleared out the dining room, arranged the chairs in a **semi-circle** and set up a comfy place for their guest to read. Mr Rimpau sat down, asked for a glass of water, and when Isy plucked up enough courage to bring it to him, he grabbed her hand for a second and quietly told her that from now on he would greet every sofa **amiably** if he ever went to one of his guest's houses again to pick up some things at his guest's request.

---

semi-circle – Halbkreis; weedy – schmächtig;
amiable – freundlich

"You'd better be careful though!" replied Isy winking. "It might just answer you!"

Then she sat down in the last row next to Amanda and listened to a chapter out of the new thriller which Mr Rimpau read as an **introduction**. It was exciting and dynamic, and made them hungry for more.

"Isn't he mad at us any more?" asked Amanda timidly.

Isy shook her head, relieved. "No. Otherwise he wouldn't have come!"

After the reading there was a really good discussion between Year Six and the writer. Mr Rimpau answered their questions about his career, his books and told them how he coped with the new conditions after losing his old publisher when the Wall came down. It seemed to be a well known fact that most of the writers in the former GDR had to **start from scratch in gaining a** firm **foothold** in the new publishing business. Other students wanted to know if he had been a Party member, how much he earned on each thriller, what his favourite book was, who his idols were, where he got his ideas from, and Mr Rimpau answered all of these questions gladly and honestly.

Year Six behaved unusually well. That might have had something to do with the fact that no one had been prepared for this visit. Anyhow, Isy didn't

---

introduction – Einführung; to start from scratch – von vorne anfangen; to gain a foothold – Fuß fassen have to feel ashamed about her classmates. Trischi also seemed to be really pleased **to take the weight off his feet**.

Saskia brought up the topic of **'violence** in schools' and they discussed this until they were red in the face. Then someone asked why Mr Rimpau didn't write teenage literature.

To everybody's surprise the writer **confessed** that he was thinking about doing just that. His future heroes were two girls who **had the courage of their convictions**. He couldn't give any details, of course, but he already had a working title. It was called 'The Calamity Queens.'

The writer was dumbfounded when the entire class burst into **raucous** laughter. **He could make neither head nor tail of it**.

Isy nudged her friend.

"Amanda," she whispered. "We're going to be famous!"

---

to take the weight off one's feet – es sich bequem machen; violence – Gewalt; to confess – gestehen; to have the courage of one's convictions – Zivilcourage besitzen; raucous – schallend, rau; He could make neither head nor tail of it – Er konnte sich keinen Reim darauf machen

Von Christamaria Fiedler bei Thienemann bereits erschienen:
Spaghetti criminale
Risotto criminale
Kürbis criminale
Popcorn criminale

Fiedler, Christamaria:
Spaghetti Crime
Aus dem Deutschen von David Fermer
ISBN 3 522 17716 9

Reihengestaltung: Birgit Schössow
Einbandillustration: Birgit Schössow
Texttypografie: Marlis Killermann
Schrift: Aldus roman und Remedy double
Satz: KCS GmbH, Buchholz/Hamburg
Reproduktion: Medienfabrik, Möglingen
Druck und Bindung: Friedrich Pustet, Regensburg

5 4 3 2 1* 05 06 07 08

Thienemann im Internet: www.thienemann.de